04
59

WITHDRAWN

D0502915

Christopher
Lowell's

if you can
dream it,
you can do it!

dream décor on a budget

CLARKSON POTTER/PUBLISHERS

NEW YORK

Copyright © 2002 by Christopher Lowell
Photographs copyright © 2002 by Douglas Hill
Illustrations by Leesa Whitten

All rights reserved. No part of this book may be reproduced or transmitted in any form or by
any means, electronic or mechanical, including photocopying, recording, or by any information
storage and retrieval system, without permission in writing from the publisher.

Published by Clarkson Potter/Publishers, New York, New York.
Member of the Crown Publishing Group, a division of Random House, Inc.
www.randomhouse.com

CLARKSON N. POTTER is a trademark and POTTER and colophon are registered trademarks
of Random House, Inc.

Christopher Lowell Management: Daniel J. Levin, Levin Entertainment Co., 532 Colorado Ave.,
Santa Monica, CA 90401

Business Management: Gerri Leonard, Sendyk & Leonard Co.

CHRISTOPHER LOWELL and CHRISTOPHER LOWELL'S SEVEN LAYERS OF DESIGN
are registered trademarks of Christopher Lowell, Inc. Any unauthorized use of these names and
images is prohibited.

For information on Christopher Lowell please visit the official Christopher Lowell website at:
www.christopherlowell.com.

Printed in Japan

Design by Maggie Hinders

Library of Congress Cataloging-in-Publication Data
Lowell, Christopher
    Christopher Lowell's If you can dream it, you can do it!: dream décor on a budget / by
Christopher Lowell.—1st ed.
    Includes index.
    1. Interior decoration—Handbooks, manuals, etc.   2. Interior decoration—Psychological
aspects.   I. Title: If you can dream it, you can do it!   II. Title.
NK2115.L8826   2002
747—dc21   2001057806

ISBN 0-609-60970-X

10 9 8 7 6 5 4 3 2 1

First Edition

acknowledgments

THIS BOOK COULD NOT HAVE HAPPENED without the hard work, dedication, and support of the following people. First, to my dedicated fans and viewers of *The Christopher Lowell Show*, thank you for your ideas, questions, and suggestions; you are my inspiration. Michael Murphy, whose continuous commitment makes everything transpire. Everyone at *The Christopher Lowell Show*, especially my producers, Elaine Perkins, Ele Sampson, Elaine Sawaya, and Dana Neillie. My editorial team of Fiona Gilsenan, Ken Winchester, and Leesa Whitten. Janet Newell, for writing the projects and for her work on the web. My staff at Christopher Lowell's Inc.; thank you for putting up with my schedule 24/7. My friend and photographer, Douglas Hill, who is always going that extra mile. Thanks to Jocelyne Borys and her team for making my ideas become a reality. Judy Gonggryp for keeping me on schedule. Sohayla Cude for talking to everyone when I am doing something else. Laura Ellegard for helping me communicate my thoughts to the viewers and fans and for filling in the cracks. All of my friends at the Discovery Channel, especially Johnathan Rodgers, Clark Bunting, Jamie Grossman-Young, Susan Murrow, and Carol LeBlanc. Gerri Leonard and our business management team at Sendyk, Leonard & Co. Lauren Shakely, Maggie Hinders, Mark McCauslin, Teresa Nicholas, Derek McNally, and all the other great people at Clarkson Potter. And lastly, many thanks to my partner and manager, Daniel J. Levin of Levin Entertainment Co.

To my mother,

JOSEPHINE CAVALERI MADDEN,

1935–1990

AS A CHILD, I lived in a self-contained, imaginary world. In this world, if I could dream it, I could be it. I learned how to play the piano on the windowsill in my bedroom. I could draw before I could talk. I entertained hundreds of make-believe friends. Together we put on shows, wrote stories, explored faraway places, carried on stimulating conversations, and dreamed—all within the confines of my bedroom. I could stare up at the clouds and be transported away. A pile of old boxes became a fortress, an open suitcase became a puppet theater, and my closet was a time machine. Puff the Magic Dragon and Old Yeller were my pets, Donna Reed was my older sister, and Fred MacMurray was my big brother. My room was my universe, and those four walls stretched to any dimension my dreams required.

My parents were dreamers, too, at a time when that word often had a derogatory connotation. They encouraged our curiosity and embraced our free spirits. We moved almost every year. They taught us that no matter where the wind blew us, our home was in our heads and our hearts. It forced us to become an observant and tightly knit family. What nourished us were our dreams, no matter how ambitious, unrealistic, or unconventional. And each time we moved, Mom would carefully pack and hand-carry familiar objects to our new home. She made sure that the first morning we woke up in a strange place, we were surrounded by familiar things. The Eskimo bark basket from our days in Alaska, the Blue Willow platter from my grandmother, the set of ship's mugs from our days living aboard our boat—all helped us reconnect the dots. These mementos had become our family's icons. They weren't important or valuable to anyone else, but they told our story.

Over the years the media began to play a more prominent role in our culture, and I watched my generation become hypnotized by conflict and chaos. With each passing year radio, television, and later the information highway bombarded us with an onslaught of "reality" pictures and impressions. As the American family structure started to deteriorate, with it went passed-down myths, icons, and legends—the stuff that dreams are made of.

I watched members of my own idealistic family buckle under the weight of this cold, hard reality. First my stepgrandfather, who died feeling the world had outgrown his optimism. His wife, disillusioned, spent her final days in seclusion, away from a world she no longer understood. My mother, after many bouts with cancer, left this planet terrified that her offspring would have to endure what she could no longer abide. On her deathbed she held me close. Her last words to me were, "Christopher, you have such talent, but you will eventually find that your greatest gift is the ability to inspire others." I had no idea at the time how prophetic those words would become. This book is in homage to her spirit.

Christopher Lowell

contents

preface

I NEVER INTENDED TO BE A TV PERSONALITY. Had you told me that my years as a classical pianist, fine artist, theatrical designer, corporate creative director, and advertising hotshot would lead me to develop and host a popular how-to show, I'd have said, "Excuse me?"

My first twenty-five years were spent in the highly competitive and self-indulgent worlds of music, art, fashion, and entertainment. Talented (and not so talented) people came and went by the thousands. First you were hot, then you were not. The fickle and voracious appetites of the American consumer, combined with corporate thirst for profits, kept me hopping. Some of my work was inspired, but most simply paid the bills. And yet as my patience with temperamental artists wore thin, my fascination with the creative process grew. For my own sanity and curiosity, I wondered why some people seemed so amazingly creative while others seemed to possess little flair. Further, why did some people exhibit staggering creative vision early on but, for whatever reason, lose it as they became adults?

I began to teach part-time at a local university. Combining what I had learned in the corporate art world with many of the psychology exercises I had studied in college, I created a course called "Creativity 101."

An amazing thing happened. At one time or another, in pursuit of this elusive thing called creativity, each and every one of my students experienced an emotional meltdown that led to a creative breakthrough. What I learned from this along with the students was that everyone, to some degree, is creative. And it is not the lack of talent but fear that is creativity's greatest enemy.

When the class came to an end, my departure from the leafy but isolated world of academia turned out to be a lucky break in disguise. In the real world there was a new and growing movement toward self-help and home improvement, and I was beginning to make some important associations. Even the word *interior* kept turning over in my mind. I watched one how-to show after another, frustrated by the confusing information and the complexity of the projects. I had been in the business for years, and even I had a hard time following the demos. I remember thinking, "Wow, you'd have to be pretty confident to tackle that project." But no one was addressing the issue of confidence. Nowhere was the phrase *self-esteem* being used. I was beginning to make the association between the interior of the home and the interior of the mind. The minute I made that connection, I knew I was on the verge of a breakthrough. Still, the crystal ball was hazy.

With what was left in my bank account I shot the pilot episode of a home-improvement show. I knew that if it didn't sell, I would be paying off creditors for years to come. With the help of a remarkable young man, Dan Levin, and after many months of hard work, our baby eventually made it to television. It debuted as *Interior Motives with Christopher Lowell.* As we watched and worried, that baby eventually grew to become *The Christopher Lowell Show.* It was a dream come true.

The ensuing five years were meteoric. Top ratings, thousands of letters, and millions of hits on the website each month all proved that we had struck a chord with our audience. We were finding ways to change not just the décor, but the lives of our viewers, and in the process, we experienced transformation ourselves. We were catapulted beyond cable by our Emmys. Spoofs on *Saturday Night Live* and *South Park;* articles in *TV Guide, The Wall Street Journal,* and the *New York Times;* even an appearance on *Who Wants to Be a Millionaire* proved that we were on the American landscape. After so many years of listening to a jaded industry tell me that there was no room in daytime television for authenticity, I felt vindicated. But I was also nervous. We worked hard as a team to not get seduced by success. We had to remind ourselves daily to remember our grass-roots beginning. I was grateful for the success, but something was still missing.

It wasn't until we went on hiatus, just after completing our sixth season, that I sat down to write this book. For years, under the banner of home improvement, we had worked hard to create an inviting place for people to gather, get motivated, and, if only in small steps, begin taking charge of something we all have in common—the home.

My first book, *Christopher Lowell's Seven Layers of Design,* was a runaway success. Now in its sixth printing, it has revolutionized how the do-it-yourselfer approaches home decorating, providing a road map to keep people on budget and out of overwhelm. It also gave me an excuse to get out across America and personally meet thousands of our viewers. This extended publicity tour touched me more than usual. I could see a hunger in the eyes of many fans who looked to me for inspiration. I heard a thousand times over how our show had motivated many of them for the first time.

I thought of my childhood, grateful for having been encouraged to dream. I was sad that those who had nurtured my dreams had long since passed, taking with them their spirit, optimism, wisdom, and courage to dream. Then it hit me. My team had worked hard for the past six years to motivate. We had been tireless in our efforts to inspire. But what we hadn't done was teach others how to dream for themselves. That hungry look in the eyes of my audience was them looking to me for their dream. What we had done as a team was to dangle this inspirational "You Can Do It" carrot in front of them. We had gotten folks motivated to inadvertently carry out *our* dreams instead of teaching them how to create dreams for themselves.

That realization led to this book. In the chapters that follow we offer practical advice, tips, and techniques. But this book is not just about the rooms we have created or remodeled. It is about the meaning behind these rooms. This digest of dreams is based on the belief that if you can dream it, you can do it! By changing your mental interiors, you have an opportunity to design your own nurturing physical space, and by doing so, you can give yourself a spiritually safe and inspired place in which to dare to dream. If we can first do it for ourselves, then maybe we might have a shot at leaving a new legacy—one that supports the dreams of our children and generations to come. This book is the introduction to that process.

part 1
the pursuit
of dreams

the creativity chip

WHAT CONVINCES US that we're not creative beings and that we lack imagination? Is it ego, the yearning to be praised, and the judgment of others? After all, we're told not to even try unless we are so obviously good at something that we'll be instantly rich and famous. "Get a real job" is the common refrain. At least that's the message we get from other people and from that two-headed dragon, the media.

Now, let's be clear. The world that the media continually shoves in our faces is real. But it's lopsided. If we see only one aspect of our world, we're bound to be influenced by that point of view. And what we decide to believe becomes our reality. In fact, any time thousands of people buy into a belief, a new reality is created. The more people who share it, the more powerful and sustaining that reality becomes. Conflict occurs when people cannot agree on the rules. That's simple enough, right?

Two of my heroes, Will and Ariel Durant, devoted their lives to proving this very point. In more than a hundred published works they examined the sweep of world history and the cycles we continue to repeat. Then they took everything they had learned and distilled it down to one small book, *The Lessons of History.* One of these lessons is that mass beliefs can build empires in one century, then destroy those empires in the next. So if we agree that the mass belief system creates a reality, then doesn't it stand to reason that by changing the belief system, we change the reality? The answer is yes. So what does this have to do with creativity?

YOU ARE CREATIVE, TOO I'VE SAID IT before and I'll say it again. We are all creative. It's innate, like breathing. The body doesn't get its inspection sticker without it. There is actually a creative mechanism literally built into our brains. Like a microchip. Honest to God!

So where is this creative chip? Well, it doesn't blink in your navel, it doesn't beep going through customs, and you won't find that it came loose and got sucked up in the vacuum. But it's there, crushed flat as a pancake maybe, and stone cold, but it's ready to be rescued. Our poor creativity! We pile upon it the burdens of the world, as well as our self-judgments and those of others.

I believe creativity was bestowed on us as an antidote to stress. But our fear of being creative blocks it. So ironically, the very thing built in to reduce stress is actually stressing us all out. "So, if that's true, who got mine?" you might ask. "Somewhere in Silicon Valley there's a talent chip with my name on it," you jest?

Wait a minute, talent is a different thing. Talent is what you earn after being creative over and over again. It's a question of practice making perfect. But even that doesn't guarantee you'll accomplish anything.

Let me give you an example. One summer, a friend invited me to stay in his wonderful house. It was stocked with artist's supplies, a fabulous studio, a potter's kiln, and a grand piano. I was in heaven—at least for the first week. I'd sit at the piano to compose, only to realize that the vision running through my head wasn't music, it was a painting. Off to the studio I went. Halfway through a painting, I realized that the form on the canvas was better realized in three dimensions. Out came the clay. Now the music came to my mind, and I found my way back to the piano. The summer was winding down and so was I, after amassing two dozen half-finished projects. When the homeowner returned, I opened the door completely frazzled. With a knowing smile, he said, "Had enough?"

He then taught me something that I have never forgotten. He said, "Having talent is one thing, but without a clear dream it is completely useless. And, nothing is sadder then creativity without focus." I had been completely self-indulgent and, although I had released a ton of creativity, I never gave it a place to land long enough to do anything worthwhile. I thought that sheer talent and good tools were all that was needed. What I had not done was clarify the dream before bringing it into reality.

Another year, while working in summer-stock theater, I met a veteran actor who had once been famous worldwide. He had accepted a small part in a Chekhov play that seemed far below his once-celebrated stature. During rehearsal I asked him, in essence, what happened? This is what he told me:

> *There was a time in my life when all I could do was dream about being an actor. It was at the epicenter of every thought. Finally the day came where I landed my first part. My performance won rave reviews and I was catapulted into stardom. But fame became my motivation rather than the dream. And before I knew it, my career slowly went on automatic pilot and stayed that way for years. My performances began to loose their passion. I had become a caricature of myself. The passion for my work was replaced with the paranoia of being a has-been. Somewhere along the way, I forgot how to dream. It wasn't until I hit bottom, when I felt I had nothing to lose, that I finally surrendered my ego, said good-bye to my fear, and allowed myself to dream again. It was my dreams that saved my life.*

Here was a man who had once been in full possession of his dreams. But due to ego and fear, he had lost focus. Fear took over the dream.

finding the creative you

TO CHANGE THE POINT OF VIEW OF OTHERS and fly in the face of an accepted reality is no small task. To go up against a mass belief system means you need to have both a powerful dream and thoughtful plans to execute it. Well, having said that, what about our smaller dreams? What about the dreams that have nothing to do with leading a nation? What about those little subconscious private and personal desires like, I'd like a better life, to be happier, to feel safer, to have a hand in my own destiny? Compared to a dream that could change the course of history, these small dreams seem rather—well, reasonable. But wait a second here. If they're that reasonable, how come there aren't thirty million Americans having amazing lives, being supremely happy, fearlessly safe, and creating their own extraordinary futures?

Could it be that even these small personal dreams also require a measure of conviction, faith, and courage to carry them out? Well, who wants even that much responsibility? Who'll risk even that much for a dream? Who's got even that kind of time? The good news is "I've got a dream." The bad news is "So, what do I do with it?"

IN MEDIEVAL TIMES, war may have surrounded many castles, but the moat and the drawbridge kept harm beyond the gates. Inside was a safe, self-contained world inhabited by all those who shared a single belief—a family, if you will, of like-minded people dreaming about a better world. This is the sense in which your home should be your castle. It's the place away from the Sturm und Drang of reality. Your walls keep out the sights and sounds of the world around you. It's your haven to dream, to create, to experiment, and to be at peace. At least it's supposed to be.

For many of us, the home was once a dream place—an icon of unlimited possibilities. But as the home changed, the environment did not. Home stopped being a place to dream or a mechanism of support. It no longer supports possibilities. It's a daily reminder that dreaming has ceased and the walls are closing in. And for many of us the home is simply a motel: a place where you check in for the night. It's just another pit stop in the rat race, or a convenient place to stash your stuff.

Why? Once again, it's all about fear. We're afraid we don't have the money or the time, and that we wouldn't know what to do to our homes even if we could. It just doesn't mean enough to risk the effort. And to top it off, to make a home a support mechanism to nurture who we want to be means we have to figure out what that is. How, pray tell, do we do that? Overloaded and overwhelmed, we retreat. We have decided that to dream isn't worth the effort. We decide that it's easier to accept the humdrum reality around us instead.

This is where your home can provide the most constructive and meaningful focus. Making your home a place that will support and nourish you—one that reflects your heart's desire—can be the most significant thing you do for yourself and your family. Because whether we like it or not, we are how we live. Everything we surround ourselves with is a direct reflection of who we were and who we currently are. In fact, so powerful is the correlation between one's mental interior and one's home interior that some of us are afraid to invite people over for fear that we might expose our real selves. Many a sitcom episode has followed this very premise.

Your home is indeed the perfect metaphor and the ideal

home is
where the
dream is

arena to get in touch with your personal creativity. It's not about decorating, painting, or buying stuff. A sofa or a lamp in and of itself won't change your life. The *meaning* behind it could, however, change everything. It's not about your fear of color; it's about fear of choosing. It's not about finding one's personal style; ultimately, it's about finding one's self. And since the home, the place where you live, should be the very center of your universe, it only makes sense to begin there.

It is within your power to make the environment you call home not just an accommodation, but a place that feeds the very essence of who you want to be. You have the opportunity to create a new reality for the future.

Home is where the dream is. And if your home is indeed a mirror of your life, then doesn't it follow that by changing your mental interior, you can change your surroundings? And, conversely, if you change your home interiors to reflect what you want to be, will your mental interior change too? The answer is a resounding yes.

a dream by any other name

OKAY, SO WHAT ARE DREAMS, ANYWAY? And why would I want to get trapped in the drama of having one of them in the first place?

Excellent questions!

A dream, in its infancy, is simply an idea. Gosh, we have lots of ideas every minute of the day. An idea certainly isn't an elaborate plan by any stretch of the imagination—it's merely a thought, a flash, a fancy. So you can get an idea without having to drag conviction, faith, and courage into it, right? Yes, you can have thousands of ideas. But ideas aren't dreams.

Let's put this into musical terms. If an idea is a single note, then the dream could be as big as Beethoven's Fifth Symphony. Or it could be as simple as the song "Happy Birthday." An idea is simply a piece of a dream. The individual notes, by themselves, mean nothing. What we do with them can and has, with the right inspiration, affected all of humanity. A part is only as good as its whole. So knock yourself out! You can have thousands of ideas. They'll rattle around in your head, take up space for a while, then get stuffed in your brain's dead-letter file. Depending on how long you're willing to ignore them, they will vanish. No one, including you, will be the wiser for it!

Think about this: Every single invention that exists on this planet was the result of someone's idea. Something as dull as a kitchen sponge may not have changed the world but it certainly seems hard to imagine our world without one. Imagine trying to get early support for this brainstorm? "So this sponge thing?

Well, it should be rectangular; it'll absorb stuff and, oh, by the way, it's currently living at the bottom of the sea. Whaddya think?"

Some ideas might have been better not acted upon at all. How about the person who invented those "popcorn" ceilings—what were they thinking? Imagine the pitch: "What's great about it is that your entire ceiling will look like cottage cheese—with sparkles!"

Well, never mind—we can all smile at someone else's predicament while emphathizing with their embarrassment. It is out of fear, or potential embarrassment, that we let our ideas stagnate. Our alternative is to live in the inherited world of everyone else's ideas. So in answer to the question "Are dreams necessary?" let me put it this way: It's like sex in a marriage; it's not mandatory, but without it the marriage can be joyless.

Locked within the center of one's dreams is one's heart's desire. Suspended somewhere between the conscious and the unconscious are our dreams. Sequestered there are the secrets of the spirit and the wellspring of our personal creativity. By not finding this secret garden we render ourselves defenseless against whatever popular mass reality exists. Armed with only our fear, we can journey through an entire lifetime without ever finding our point of distinction—the very fingerprint of who or why we were even here. Or even more frustrating, we start dreaming so late in our lives that we run out of time. Spending your life without personal joy, unable to feel and implement your heart's desire, to me is the ultimate tragedy.

DREAMING WITH YOUR HEART DREAMS ARE FLEXIBLE: They can be changed at a moment's notice with no questions asked. And you can dream anywhere and at any time. Dreaming is not for the sleep-deprived, however; that kind of night dreaming is usually disorienting and often fueled more by our anxieties than our inspirations. So, if you need rest, take a nap. Creative dreaming is more meditative. When done effectively a good session of dreaming can get the blood running and excite the imagination. But if it is ignored or repressed, dreaming will flicker out like a candlewick.

So how do we reach this creative plane? Therapy? No, that's far too intellectual. Dreams are a matter of the heart—the center of how and what we feel. Just simply relax and meditate. You don't have to go to an ashram or form a human chain. This is not a religion, a cult, or a parlor game. It's just you thinking about your heart's desire.

What you are doing is creating your own personal sense of reality that will be your spiritual space to dream in. The longer you consider your heart's desires, the more ideas you'll get. Beware: The part of your brain that's been in charge these many years might get a little territorial, even try to sabotage your dreaming by persuading you that your dreams are unrealistic flights of fancy. "Snap out of it, you look childish, what if someone hears you?" It's the equivalent of your own head telling you to get a real job. That's when you need a little faith. The only antidote to fear is creating a place where dreams rule. I call it the Faith Place.

When the same ideas keep circling back through over and over again, they become inspirations. These inspirations, at the moment, are not to be acted on physically. They are simply considerations—possibilities. Think of them as creative prayers. Left unfocused, these ideas will evaporate unless they have something concrete to be attracted to; what we are talking about attracting them to is your physical surroundings.

The interiors depicted in this book are living proof that creative dreaming works. They were all inspired by ideas that erupted into fully blown dreams, then finally resulted in fully manifested environments. That's how a fully resolved dream becomes a dreamscape. And that dreamscape is your home.

theme your dream

EVERY DREAM, LIKE EVERY GOOD ROOM, NEEDS A THEME. And every dream, like every good room, needs a purpose. Since I can assume by now you understand that you are how you live and that making your physical interior a support mechanism is vital, then that's where we begin. Agreed?

Good. Our goal here is to dream about an environment that will support the person you want to be, a place that can become the center of your universe—a home. Now this is no time to be practical. Right now, it's not about money, skills, or square footage. This is no time to take inventory of what you think you can't have. Right now, it's all about your head, your life, your time on this planet—dare to dream.

Let's pick a theme. This will help provide focus. To help arrive at this launching point, ask yourself these fourteen questions. Bear in mind that your answers should be your heart's desire, not your head's.

The Dream Questionnaire

1. *If you could live anywhere in the world, where would it be?* Pick a place. Now picture what you think that looks like. Is it town, country, city, or shore? Where is this place? Even if you can't pinpoint a geographical location, describe it to yourself.

_____

2. *If you could be anything you wanted when you "grow up," what would it be?* Your answer does not have to be a profession that exists or one for which you already have the skills. Pay no attention to age or physical limitation. You could be a movie star, a nurse, or a lion tamer. Go for it!

_____

3. *What makes you feel safe, cozy, and protected?* If you can't put your finger on an exact situation, try describing the feeling to yourself.

_____

4. *What does "pampering" mean to you?* Where are you and how do you feel when you are completely pampered?

_____

5. *If you could acquire only one object, what would it be?* This is your icon. It doesn't have to be practical, life-supporting, or even real. Just choose something, from a piece of bamboo to a wing chair to a doohickey thingie.

_____

6. *What is the sound you most love to hear?* Water, children playing, a lawn mower, singing? What sound brings a smile to your face at just the thought of it?

_____

7. *What is the personal quality of human beings that you admire above all else?* This does not have to be a quality you think you possess.

_____

8. *If you could, what one thing would you do every day to make yourself feel pampered and indulged?* This one shouldn't be too hard to answer!

_____

9. *If you could have someone handle three small tasks in your life, what would they be?* Each task can be as small as emptying the dishwasher or as important as daily shopping or driving you to work.

_____

10. *Think of a color.* Don't think about it, just see it. The color does not have to be your favorite—just the first thing that comes to mind.

_____

11. *What trait do you most admire about yourself?* "My ability to _____

_____."

12. *What is the most courageous thing you've ever done—no matter how small?*

_____

13. *What was the happiest moment of your life to date?* This does not mean the most important.

_____

14. *What one thing that you've done for yourself makes you most proud?* This can be very private and need not be life-changing.

_____

To show you how these questions can tell you about your desires and help elicit some creative dreams, I took the test myself. Here are my answers.

1. If you could live anywhere in the world, where would it be?
   By the shore. I've always wanted to live right on the beach in a European country like Italy.

2. If you could be anything you wanted when you "grow up," what would it be?
   Beyond doing exactly what I'm doing now, I'd like to be the person who convinces the American public school system that Creative Dreaming should be mandatory in the curriculum beginning in the first grade. I'd like to unlock the creative potential in young kids while giving them the necessary tools to maintain the skill throughout their lives.

3. What makes you feel safe, cozy, and protected?
   Being in an upscale tropical-style hotel with all the amenities, where everyone knows me and protects me. It should be in a quaint coastal European town where everyone understands English and everything is within walking distance so I don't have to drive.

4. What does "pampering" mean to you?
   A white fluffy robe, laid out on a down-filled bed. Opposite is a VCR and a stack of video biographies from A&E and a huge all-night room-service menu. Also, living at my grandmother's house and waiting for my stepgrandfather to tuck me into the eighteenth-century canopy bed with the red toile hangings. As he turned out the light, he'd sit there and recite Shakespeare to me.

5. If you could acquire only one object, what would it be?
   A state-of-the-art laptop that comes with a full piano keyboard, an intense graphic package, and a DVD player.

6. What is the sound you most love to hear? Ocean waves.

7. What is the personal quality of human beings that you admire above all else? Talent.

8. If you could, what one thing would you do every day to make yourself feel pampered and indulged?
   Have dinner magically arrive on a bed tray every night, then disappear by the morning.

9. If you could have someone handle three small tasks in your life, what would they be?
   Empty my trash cans, put gas in my car, and replace any toiletries when empty.

10. Think of a color. Terra-cotta.

11. What trait do you most admire about yourself? My ability to inspire others.

12. What is the most courageous thing you've ever done—no matter how small?
    Creating the Christopher Lowell project with no money.

13. What was the happiest moment of your life to date?
    Doing the very first CL show, when I looked in the camera for the first time with a lump in my throat and said, "Hi, everybody, I'm Christopher Lowell."

14. What one thing that you've done for yourself makes you most proud? Surrendering my life to be whatever God needs.

Having reviewed my answers, did you learn anything about me? And what could this mean in terms of my dreams? Here's what I learned:

Answer 1 tells me that I get rejuvenation from the water. Given my druthers, I'd love to be by the ocean. I might not be able to afford beachfront property, but could I have the illusion of being at the shore?

Answer 2 tells me that I need an environment that will support my ability to work on my life's path. I need to have a communication center that is also a creative space.

Answer 3 addresses safety. I like a tropical feeling similar to a resort. People know me and are there to protect my privacy, so I feel a secluded environment will nurture me more then wide-open spaces. Visually, I am stimulated by a European sensibility, but I must be able to communicate. I would prefer to walk rather then drive. This probably speaks to my need for community and, to a certain extent, a need for continuity.

Answer 4 suggests to me that I have a fascination with observing people, peeking into their lives, and that I'm curious about how the decisions people make directly impact their lives. Because it is harder for me to blend into the background these days, the bedroom is the room in which I prefer to spend time, and the TV is one way for me to observe individuals' lives. The white fluffy bathrobe indicates to me that comfort is essential to my feeling pampered. I love the idea of room service because I am ceremonial about taking my meals, but having them brought into the bedroom means I can stay in my world without interruption. The canopy bed at my grandmother's house enveloped me, making me feel safe, cozy, and valued. My grandfather's voice also suggests the art of communication.

In my answer to question 5, the object I chose is also a communication device. While I love solitude, I don't want isolation. I need a tool to help me express myself, which I do through art, writing, and music. This could suggest a work environment that feels more home than office.

Answer 6 is again about my love for the sound of water.

Answer 7 speaks to admiration of people who exhibit their creativity, and makes it obvious why I like to be surrounded with manifestations of it.

In answer 8, food becomes a central theme. And the bedroom for me is central headquarters. It also says that I prefer the world to come into my reality rather than venturing out into it myself.

Answer 9 suggests that a full trash can reminds me of clutter. Organization is important to me. Everything should be in its place. Not wanting to put gas in the car is just one more excuse for me not to drive. Here again, this tells me that I don't want to venture into the reality of the world if I don't have to. Shopping for bathroom toiletries is something I hate. I don't like to spend time on necessities—I'd rather spend my time in creative pursuits!

Answer 10: Terra-cotta reminds me of my trips to Italy, a painting by Rembrandt, and the earth. It's a color that connects me back to nature.

Answer 11 reflects that my ability to inspire is my life's work. My environment is the breeding point for me to think about life and to dream. But I also need inspiration in order to inspire others.

Answer 12 reveals that I am a risk-taker. That much of my self-worth is connected to my ability to create and to meet challenges. This also tells me that I get bored easily. I need to be doing something at all times.

Answer 13 tells me that against all odds, I did what I dreamed of—that I have a platform that could be a part of my life for a long time. This also means I have a responsibility to practice what I preach and stay clear and focused. My home must reflect the Christopher Lowell I hope to be.

Answer 14 reminds me that I must continue to reach out in faith—to be an instrument, a projection screen, and an example to those around me. To make sure that the choices I make are responsible. And that I find a way to enroll others in a dream that God wants, not one that I think will make me happy.

So to sum up what my answers tell me, I learn that I want a home that is very organized and deliberate. Because I prefer to bring people into my dream world rather than to venture out, I need a sanctuary that promotes creativity. A place that makes me feel private but not lonely. A place that is well kept but not formal. A place where the world is kept at bay by the sounds of water, and that has light dancing on terra-cotta walls. It should be as maintenance-free as possible. And I am happier in a home that is theatrical rather than trendy, more classic than elegant, and that offers privacy rather than exposure.

There—now it's your turn!

WHEN I FIRST BEGAN STUDYING THE ANSWERS from my questionnaire, my goal was to focus my dreamscape, so I paid close attention to words I used.

My answers put heavy emphasis on the bedroom so that's where I decided to concentrate my dream. I would allow myself to go through the dream process and create a prototypical Christopher Lowell bedroom. To begin with, I compiled a list of meaningful words based on my answers—considerations, if you will:

As I concentrated on this growing list, the words began to trigger other con-

siderations. For instance, the shore was clearly my dream destination. But, to my surprise, I had no mental images that suggested sand, boats, or anything else remotely connected to a day at the beach. In fact, in my mind the beach was actually in the distance. I imagined myself high on a bluff overlooking a tropical coastline. I was in some kind of open-air structure made of bamboo poles and a deep plum-colored fabric. It reminded me of cabanas at hotels where guests can get an out-of-doors spa treatment.

I would have felt self-conscious in this reverie if I had not concentrated on the hypnotic pounding of the waves. It was that one imagined sound, above all, that had somehow became my catalyst and transported me back into my almost meditative state. Overhead, the fabric undulated, its gold-tasseled braid caught a gentle breeze as it fluttered in the warm gusts of salt-laden air. I could see torches being lit at dusk and ancient gilded Asian masks suspended against the deep indigo night. The sound of the waves spoke to me so clearly that I knew it was time to manifest that idea—that is, take it from inside my head and bring it into the world around me. But how?

Back to reality, I thought of record stores, where there were CDs of natural sounds available. Of course! Or better yet, how about a sound machine? It would play nonstop and I wouldn't have to change the CD ever! I promptly bought one,

took it home, placed it in my empty room, then closed my eyes. Like magic, again I was literally transported back to that same place on the bluff by the tranquil rhythm of the ocean. Propelled by success, with sound machine cranked, I drifted off to sleep. My journey had begun.

REALIZING THE DREAM

THE NEXT DAY, the alarm slapped reality in my face and life offered its customary distractions. I kept my journey to myself, knowing that my commitment couldn't yet survive anybody else's disapproval. I remember thinking that it was like being in the infancy of a love affair—the secret was part of the romance.

That evening as I glanced at my icon list, both the words *bamboo* and *orchid* jumped out at me. Coincidentally, I had just received the gift of a long-stemmed orchid. A bamboo stick supported the plant. Picking up the pot and staring at the flower, I imagined myself at the foot of a giant orchid, with a supporting trellis rising up about 8 feet behind me. Then it hit me: This was the organic element I was searching for. I would be just like the folks on Gilligan's Island—making clever things out of bamboo. Whimsical, yes, but I wondered if this one element might spur even more ideas. I had to have a piece of bamboo.

At a nearby import store, I asked the saleswoman where they got their display bamboo. She laughed and told me that she got it from a catalog she'd seen on *my* show. Indeed one of my guests, Sandi Reinke, had a catalog called Loose Ends. I resolved to check the catalog immediately.

As I was leaving the import store, two masks against a wall caught my eye. At first I thought I was imagining it, but, for less than $40, I had two more of my dream objects—icons that supported my dream.

Sure enough, the Loose Ends catalog sold bamboo. As I looked at the various sizes and shapes available, I began to dream of actually making a bed frame out of it. I sketched and sketched, but to no avail. It was too complicated and I couldn't get the design right. A setback loomed. Had I been too ambitious? Like an evil genie, the Voice of Reason echoed in my head, "Get a real job." Feeling sheepish about being caught up in a daydream, I was ready to completely give up the bamboo bed idea. "Imagine, Christopher Lowell, sitting on a cockamamy bluff, listening to a sound machine, stroking bamboo, and looking at two Asian masks. Wake up, dream boy!"

But wait a minute. This was my life and my dream. No sooner did I shake off the Voice of Reason than a piece of paper fluttered out of the catalog. "Special," it read, "Bamboo canopy bed."

From here on it was all about faith. My mind, however, kept playing peanut gallery. "You can't sleep on a sound machine," said the voice. "Try hanging your clothes on an Asian mask," it snickered. "This is a bedroom, dream boy, get real!" I turned back to my answers. What about that computer? What about that eat-in-bed fantasy? Was that really my heart's desire? What about the TV? What about my clothes, my books, my videotapes? Defeated, I went to bed.

I tossed and turned all night. My Asian masks had become predators that were chasing me through a thick forest of black bamboo. Tina Louise kept throwing orchid blossoms, blinding my eyes while the menacing roar of the ocean threatened to consume me. I awoke burdened with a hangover of defeat. There were my little icons placed around the floor looking more like spies than the refuge of future dreams I had imagined.

FINDING WITHOUT SEEKING HOPING FOR DISTRACTION and to salvage some goodness from my misery, I decided to visit a sick friend. When I got to the hospital, my friend was finishing her lunch. We chatted for a moment but she could tell I was distracted. She was right. Her bed tray fascinated me; it had a swing arm and a foot that slid under the bed on castors. That bed tray was cool. Ugly, but practical. I started to think back to the bamboo bed; its rails went almost to the floor. The only way to have a tray was to actually make one the entire width of the bed—one that would fit over the frame itself. Nurses came and went, and my friend was delighted and satisfied that I'd come. But I derived further satisfaction from knowing that my dreamscaping had been reignited. Now I knew it was time to get going.

BRINGING THE DREAM TO LIFE I BEGAN to break down the task, organizing my work into my Seven Layers of Design. I painted the bedroom walls plum with gold trim and ordered bamboo to face two bookcases, which would flank the bed. Layer Number One, Paint and Architecture, was done. With the bed in place I chose the linens and the accessory fabrics. The purple and gold fabric added a luster to the bed and walls, making the room feel exotic and cozy. Layers Three and Four were com-

During

ABOVE LEFT Masks against indigo walls. **OPPOSITE** The dream has become a reality.

plete. But to make the bed table, I needed help. My friend Steve had a great idea: "Make it out of PVC pipe." He showed me how to achieve a faux bamboo technique with hot glue and spackle. The bed tray, now an entire rollaway table, slipped neatly over the bed frame and is now my favorite object. With caned side tables and additional bamboo pieces, Layer Five had brought function to the space. The Asian masks now floated against a backdrop of lavender paint. At the end of the bed suspended fabric shades, illuminated from within, cast a torch-light glow. White orchids basked in the flicker of candlelight, and uplights sent dramatic shadows dancing through live bamboo plants. And in the distance, the sound of crashing waves transported what once was an empty space to that tropical bluff overlooking the sea.

What began as a simple dream based on my heart's desire had flourished into three-dimensional reality—my own private Balinese retreat. My evening meal may not magically appear on my bed tray, but I have eaten many a meal in bed, watching biographies and writing this book. And, when necessary, I can always call on the distant roar of the ocean to send me off on yet another dream.

This room was so full of ideas that we loved, we went ahead and re-created it in our showcase house, one of the many homes we redo each season. You may recognize this room from my first book. But now you know how the meaning behind it changed my life!

So, as you look through the makeovers in the following pages, don't just admire what others have done. Let these rooms inspire you to transform your own home. If there's one thing I know, it's this: *You Can Do It!*

Part 2
dreams
come true

one-room wonders

In our multitasking, always-strapped-for-space lives,

we often have rooms that must serve double or

even triple duty. On the following pages,

you'll see how the art of furniture

placement can create a

complete home all in

small

function

SIMPLICITY

one room. You'll also learn how you can interrupt a space to create several different living environments. That works well for those who have too little room. But suppose you have a main living room that's larger than a studio. Are you really using it to its full potential? The first makeover illustrates how you can get the most out of the space you have.

rooms
within
rooms

one room
in four

MAKING A SPACE SOCIABLE THIS ROOM HAD A FIREPLACE, a window, and a door on one wall, a very large arched window on another, and a dining room arch on yet another wall. It was literally full of holes. All these openings needed to be united in some way to compensate for their various shapes and sizes. Our solution came from a feature in the room itself. Beside the fireplace were a series of stair-steps designed to hold objects. These flared elements, with their tile tops, became our inspiration. We made six flared boxes with square plywood tops, leaving the inside hollow to add a removable pole on a cup and dowel. After faux-finishing them, we placed one on either side of each opening at exactly the same height, to act as decorative corbels from which we could later cascade fabric panels.

The symmetrical vertical lines would help even out the height discrepancy among the openings.

We painted the room in a warm but deep yellow gold. This not only added color to the space but helped to minimize the contrast between the walls and the very heavy dark wood ceiling. The treatment actually made the room seem taller. Now Layers One and Two were complete. Since this apartment dweller loves to entertain, our next goal was to maximize every inch of seating possible.

Here is where I need to remind you that the average human form needs only between 18 and 20 inches to comfortably move in and around furniture. When clustering pieces into groupings, also remember that keeping the furniture low allows everyone seated to have a clear view of the room from almost every angle. We knew that later we'd put an area rug in front of the fire, so this would now be the first focal seating group. Between the fireplace and the front door we put a full-size sofa, which still left enough room for a sofa table. Once merchandised, this would also act as a foyer area so that guests coming in the front door wouldn't just land in the room. And it created a new surface to which an occasional chair could be drawn up. Most important, this area was now ideal for task lighting.

We went on to concentrate on our window treatments, adding rich pumpkin tapestry panels to give that touch of old-world Spanish. The corbels also add an architectural feature to the room. How's that for dual function?

Once the furniture was clustered into connected islands, the walls were free for storage and placement of art. Remember, without storage and hard surfaces, rooms are less livable and don't work. With this in mind, we added a small

Before

ABOVE RIGHT Across from the sofa we placed a backless settee. This is what I always refer to as a cross-linking device. By placing a piece with two different seating aspects here, we could add two more club chairs on the far side. This allows people to sit back-to-back on either side, creating essentially two complete conversation areas. Oh, and the club chairs swivel, so that those seated can turn to look out the window or have a private conversation. By now we had seating for ten people in an average-size room. Too cool. Swinging wrought-iron doors are in keeping with the Spanish antique look of this room.

barrel table between each of the club chairs and an oversize coffee table between the settee and the sofa. We chose a glass-topped table so that the lovely pattern of the floral area rug showed through. Next we found a reproduction bamboo hutch that gave the room an eclectic, well-traveled feeling and, more important, became the new home for an unattractive stereo unit (it could also house a TV). We like the fact that it was decorative storage. And it was also the proper scale to balance out the height of the fireplace opposite it. This created two high points in balance with the space; we'd merchandise them later. Oh my! There was still room for two more chairs. These are actual recliners, thank you very much. Against the mirrored wall at the opposite end of the room we had space for yet another seating area. Here we placed a round tufted ottoman which can be drawn up to the sofa table and to the coffee table, too. With a basket on it, it can even double as a mail holder. Who knew?

Accessorizing the space was the fun part. With so much to work with, we knew less was best. And now that our furniture was mostly low, we needed to find ways to create unobtrusive height in the room. On the sofa table, a cluster of modern sculptural containers did the trick. Elsewhere, candlesticks added height. A few overscale objects dispersed evenly around the room made for great still lifes without adding room "dandruff" that would steal living space. Monochromatic prints elongated the arched window, while matching watercolors

in giant overscale frames added drama and balance flanking our bamboo hutch. And finally we added tall plants, again for height, as well as some smaller ones atop each corbel.

The color scheme in this room is monochromatic, yet runs from rust through deep peach into light honey. When complete, four new areas were defined in the space. But what I like best about this room is that it's classic—everything can be moved and it's an inventory of furniture that can last forever. And even though the owner has space for plenty of partygoers in one room, her favorite spot is resting against the settee in front of the open fire. Sounds good to me.

LEFT Candles always add a special touch to a room's lighting. If you entertain, make sure to have plenty of candlelight. It's flattering to food and to faces. **TOP** These built-in features inspired our window treatments. To avoid a regimented look, we placed similar but individual pieces on each shelf, picking up the color of the tile fragments along the way. **ABOVE** We wanted to balance out the low scale of the furniture without being obtrusive. Tall candlesticks on the coffee table serve this purpose.

MANHATTAN MAGIC THIS REPLICATED STUDIO is a great example of how you can make your indoor space a reflection of your heart's desires. Can you imagine turning a single room into four entirely separate living areas? Well, that's just what we did here. The room's success as a design lies in its basic arrangement of spaces. But what makes this room's inhabitant truly feel at home is the soothing monochromatic color scheme—muted paint colors and crisp fabric slipcovers. It's a minimalist look that reflects the pared-down, sophisticated image we wanted to illustrate.

four rooms in one

Big-city dwellers in places like Manhattan may have the world at their feet, but chances are their first apartment is barely bigger than a shoe closet! If you find yourself in such circumstances, don't bemoan the lack of space, find ways to maximize it. The key to efficiency living is to create rooms within rooms by figuring out what essential tasks and activities you'll need to accommodate. Then you can begin the process of "breaking up the space."

What we did first was to divide the space into four separate living areas: an office, a bedroom, a dressing room, and a living room. But this was a challenge: The space was a simple rectangle with a bay window at one end. It had a small bathroom and a closet, but no vanity area and no storage. Nor was there a place to cook, check e-mail, or watch television.

We got around the room's deficiencies by facing and accepting the bottom line of one-room living—the bed is likely to be the single largest object in the room. Your first instinct might be to try to conceal or disguise the most intimate piece of furniture you own, but after all, a bed is a bed—so play it up! We turned this potential eyesore into a problem solver by making the bed the centerpiece of the room. It became a fantasy island and it opened the way for us to create four completely different environments—a problem turned profitable.

Centering the bed as the focal point not only freed up the surrounding wall area, but also presented some opportunities for modular storage by incorporating two room dividers and several sets of shelves into one unit. (You'll find step-by-step instructions on how to build

OPPOSITE Very little light penetrates to the back of this room, and vanity areas must be well lit to serve their purpose. Two lamps on such a small shelf might be overwhelming in another situation, but they are put to good use here. Containers are filled with toiletries such as shampoo and lotion, making these mundane items more attractive. A folding screen in the corner of the room can shield the vanity from view and provide privacy for changing if a surprise guest drops by for that spur-of-the-moment date.

this bed on page 44.) We put a clever "porthole" into the headboard wall to let light flow throughout the room from the big bay window. After all, who wants to sleep in a dark cave? This three-quarter wall and the half-wall footboard define the spaces in the room, maintaining privacy without enclosing the bed in a claustrophobic box.

To accommodate the need for a dressing area, the back of the footboard became a vanity simply by installing a shelf and a mirror directly onto the half wall. For the "living room," we transformed the bay window, truly the room's most outstanding natural feature, into a valuable seating area. Facing it is a coffee table and a comfy loveseat. A rolling cart pushed up to a hanging side-loaded magazine cache cleverly conceals a TV and a stereo. All the functional stuff in this room is hidden but, in reality, it's right there when it's needed.

ABOVE AND RIGHT The seating area offers glimpses of the room beyond, but it is easy to forget that a full-size bed lies behind the wall. Against the wall-mounted light box on the left is a roll-around table that seats four for dinner and doubles as a roomy workspace for multitasking. Love that!

manhattan bed

ALL-IN-ONE SLEEPING AND STORAGE

Like many of our large pieces, this bed is based on a box platform that forms the centerpiece of the construction. Two semiwalls complete the bed at either end. You can use inexpensive core doors for this purpose, but a frame built of 1-by-4s is sturdier. We covered our footboard with fabric tied at the corners and gave our headboard a faux-linen finish.

Approximately four 4-by-8-foot sheets
   ¾-inch plywood
1 sheet wiggle board
Eight 4-by-8-foot sheets ¼-inch ply-
   wood
1-by-4-inch pine boards
Wood glue
Wood screws
Finishing nails
Sandpaper and sander
Wood putty
Table saw
Jigsaw
Power drill and screwdriver
Safety glasses
Tape measure and pencil

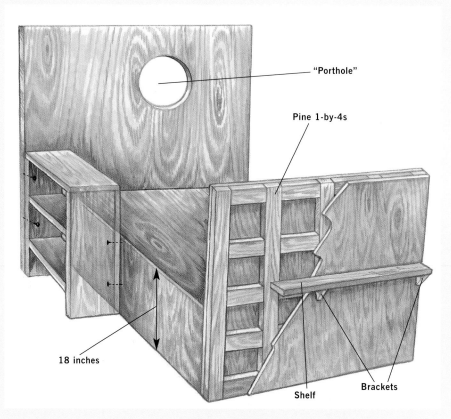

"Porthole"

Pine 1-by-4s

18 inches

Brackets

Shelf

1. Construct a box for the bed out of ¾-inch plywood, 18 inches high and 1 inch larger all around than the mattress dimensions. For extra strength, add 2 vertical plywood braces parallel to the top and bottom. If you prefer using both a mattress and box springs, adjust the height of the platform accordingly so that the top of the mattress is approximately 23 inches off the floor.

2. Construct a headboard out of 1-by-4-inch pine framing sandwiched between 2 pieces of ¼-inch plywood. Secure with wood glue and wood screws. Before assembling the headboard, cut a "porthole" circle slightly off-center in both pieces of ¼-inch plywood at the desired height using a jigsaw. Attach the headboard to the top of the bed platform with wood screws.

3. Using the same ¾-inch plywood, construct a bookcase with 3 shelves approximately 30 inches high, 28 inches wide, and the depth of the distance between the edge of the bed platform and the edge of the headboard. Screw the bookcase to both the headboard and the bed platform to secure the headboard vertically.

4. Build a footboard using the same pine framing sandwiched between 2 pieces of ¼-inch plywood. If desired, add a shelf on the back of the footboard to serve as a vanity. Mark the outside of the footboard to correspond with the horizontal framing and attach shelf brackets through the plywood to the framing supports.

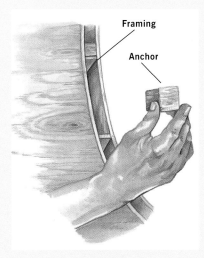

Framing

Anchor

5. For a finished inside edge to the port-hole, cut the wiggle board the width of the thickness of the head-board. (Wiggle board is scored on one side, making it flexible.) Secure with wood glue and finishing nails. If necessary, cut small pieces of wood for anchors to insert between the plywood pieces around the hole for attaching the wiggle board.

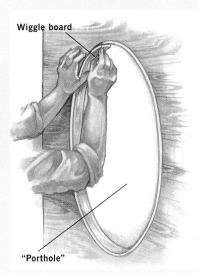

Wiggle board

"Porthole"

tricks to make the most of one-room living

- Look for unused space and capitalize on existing elements.
- You've heard me say it before: If you can't build out, build up. Build shelves all the way up to the ceiling and get a folding stepstool so you can reach to the top.
- Believe it or not, putting lots of little things in a little space actually makes it look even smaller. Avoid clutter and select the few large-scale items you'll really need.
- Build rooms within rooms. Efficient "space breakers" can result in separate environments for different activities.
- Use half walls, screens, fabric dividers, blocks of wall color, or just different furniture groupings to distinguish one environment from another.
- Think up clever storage ideas: shelves built into the bed, racks that fold flat against the wall, or storage units that roll underneath other pieces.
- Find ways to bring lots of light into the space. Dark corners are visually wasted space. If there is no natural light, create it. For instance, in this room, the illumination tower by the sofa is simply five white lampshades threaded over a dowel wrapped with Christmas lights.
- It's an old trick, but mirrors can really work wonders, visually doubling or even tripling a room's dimensions.

on with the show

FAUX

illusion

rich colors

stage

Although I didn't realize it at the time, the years I

spent working in the theater were preparation for

my future role as a designer. After all, what I do is

add drama to people's homes, and then teach it on

TV. But when you think about it, your home really

is like the world of the stage or the cinema. You set

it by adding mood, drama, lighting, and dressing.

It tells the story of who you are

and who you want to

be. If you've

followed your

life's script well, when the

audience arrives—I mean, when

company arrives—they'll give your

production rave reviews. But

remember, the most important audience

is you.

D R A M A

theater living

ALL THE WORLD'S A STAGE THE HOMEOWNER OF THIS SPACE works as a celebrity hair designer. He wanted a dramatic room where both he and his clients would be comfortable. Once he cast me in the role of set designer, it was my job to help him interpret his life's script.

To begin Act One, I first examined the bones of the existing space. One side of the room was dominated by a huge 15-foot Spanish-style window. Its graceful arch immediately reminded me of the proscenium arch above a stage. After painting the room a rich dusty green, we decided to have our friend Jeff Raum heighten this effect by stenciling an elaborate rococo border around the window. Ah, the theater!

On either side of the fireplace two small windows cried out for a dramatic touch. We installed thick cornices over them, and used paint to simulate gold leaf. Now, don't they remind you of those VIP box seats that flank turn-of-the-century opera houses? We loved the gold so much, we continued it as the trim all around the room. Such drama!

With the backdrop complete, we then turned our attention to the set's décor. Layer Three, Upholstered Furniture, gave us the opportunity to feature some velvet jewel-tone supporting pieces. These whimsical classics reminded us of the old horse-hair chairs found in vintage theater lobbies. When I say keep these high-ticket upholstered pieces neutral, this proves that it doesn't mean beige! We added accent fabric in the form of a rich red Oriental rug that belonged to the owner. The pattern of the carpet inspired us to hang tapestry drapes on the windows. Intermission. Curtain.

The final act concentrates on the most-often-ignored layer of decorating: lighting. My days in the theater taught me that without light, the show cannot go on. If you want to add intimacy and create interesting patterns of light and shadow, as much illumination should be coming from the floor as from the ceiling. In addition to our torchères, we installed decorative Fortuny lamps and show-stopping uplights. At night, these not only exaggerate the shadows around the room, but are also reminiscent of stage footlights. Applause. Fade to black.

OPPOSITE By clustering the furniture around the fireplace, we left valuable wall space free to add storage and great wall art.

Before

RIGHT We loved the tapestry drapes so much that we continued them over the top of the window. Actually, it's another illusion of the theater. The top drape is faux, just like the border. Got you again!

TIP When adding intense color to any space, make sure it's spread evenly around the room to create a balance. Here, a fabulous retro poster brings the red up from below, drawing the eye overhead. The scale tells it all—go bigger!

moroccan mystique

IN-HOME ENTERTAINING SHOULD BE FUN, right? Well, for many of us, the idea of inviting people over to see how we really live can actually be a bit intimidating. I've received so many letters from viewers asking, "How can I create an environment where my guests can relax and enjoy themselves?" Well, guess what? By creating an environment where you can relax and enjoy yourself. If you're proud of your surroundings, you'll be at ease and so will your guests.

In fact, I can't think of a more important place to go all out than the dining room. Think of your favorite restaurant. Fifty percent of your experience there has nothing to do with the food—rather, it's the atmosphere. And in most restaurants, that atmosphere is heightened by a theme. So, take a tip from the pros and implement one at home with your own dream dining room.

The owner of this house wanted to duplicate the experience he had at a Moroccan restaurant he often frequents, but he was afraid to try to create a true fantasy room. We decided to step up to the challenge and show him how easy it could be to make his dream come true. We imagined the room filled with deep, rich colors and flickering lights and one elaborate feature that would make it a true desert oasis—a tented ceiling.

It may seem a far cry from the "before" picture to an Arabian Nights fantasy, but if you look more closely at the room, you'll see several existing elements that already evoke this theme. First of all, the room has some suggestions of age: the slightly distressed plaster and the wrought-iron chandelier, which we thought was quite fabulous. Next, the room's coved ceiling already suggested a tent. Even the arched entrance to the room seemed ideal. The owner had indoor-outdoor wrought-iron furniture with details that simply needed embellishment. And we loved the existing granite shelf supported by two aged-looking stone corbels— we just needed to play it up as another focal point. So, while the materials said, "I'm aged and full of character," the austerity of the space said, "Help, I'm afraid to express myself!"

So what's missing here? Now that we had a theme, we needed to find ways to add color through paint and fabric, and to add drama, with floor-to-ceiling scale. We began with Layer One, Paint and Architecture. We painted the walls a deep cinnamon color from the Christopher Lowell Designer Paint Collection, Clay Cotta. To play up the domed ceiling and chandelier, we selected a Middle

Before

OPPOSITE The plain chandelier became a true focal point of this room, with a little help from the fabric store. In the end, we hung almost 70 yards of fabric around the room. Because the fabric is pulled back to the corners, the whole room appears to be draped, not just half of it.

Eastern–inspired lightweight corduroy fabric in an Indian rug motif. With a combination of 2-inch closet dowels and four PVC plumbing elbows, we constructed a rectangle with the same dimensions as the glass tabletop. Eight panels of fabric were fitted onto the rectangle. The canopy is suspended from chains that are attached to the ceiling with pothooks and then attached to the dowels with eye hooks, similar to the way we hang our suspended bed canopies.

As a visual connecting device, we added a valance in a matching striped fabric. This was simply stapled to lathing strips and secured to the wall with finishing nails. But it's the tent-flap detail that really sells the illusion. This fabric panel is attached with Velcro to the PVC-and-dowel rectangle to create a sus-

Before

RIGHT Capitalize on existing details whenever possible in your room redos. The dated plaster wall treatment and funky curves and arches of this room actually worked in our favor. Those suggestions of antiquity created the authenticity of our desert Casbah theme.

pended ceiling effect. To warm up the floor, we took an existing Oriental rug from the adjoining living room, bringing the room's ornate patterns and matching colors underfoot. Luxury!

When we got to Layer Four, we turned back to fabric again, this time for accents. We took the same fabric we found for the tent ceiling and used it not only for throw pillows but also to create the chairback runners. To ensure that guests will want to linger after dinner, we added comfortable cushions to the chairs. Remember, it doesn't matter how fabulous the couscous is; if your guests are squirming around on a metal grid, that's all they'll remember of the evening.

There were just a few other special effects needed to complete the look. The stone shelf was somewhat out of scale with the room, so we visually "raised" it by placing tall torchères on either side. More important, we put a mirror behind it. This takes advantage of the large window on the other side of the room by reflecting it for facing guests, effectively doubling the space and the interest in the room. I really didn't like being able

to see into the kitchen, so we hung an import-store bead curtain in the doorway and draped more fabric behind it. Finally, we found a wonderful wrought-iron gate and used it as the finishing touch to disguise the opening. Don't forget you can always bring outdoor objects inside to help complete a look.

Lighting is crucial in a theatrical setting like this. Here, we clustered plenty of candles around the room and dressed up the chandelier with shades to soften the effect of bare bulbs. Another trick was to place an uplight behind the large urn against the far wall. This dramatizes the object as separate from the background and emphasizes the deep wall color. With all of these details in place, the owner of this room had the flickering lights and sumptuous atmosphere he had longed for.

Often what looks complicated and elaborate is really so easy once you know how it's done. With a dream to propel you forward, you are only limited by fear. So lighten up and dare to dream.

ABOVE Adding throw pillows and runners to the chairs ensures comfort as well as drama.

martini lounge

ROOM FOR THE RAT PACK WHAT DO YOU DO when your house has a room that seems too small to serve any useful purpose? One that's too cramped for a playroom but too big to be used just for storage? Hey, don't rush to judgment. By giving up those out-of-the-way nooks and crannies, you're robbing yourself of precious living space. I say, start thinking big!

This itty-bitty room sat neglected because the owner had no clue what to do with it. Yet he also said that he wanted an intimate entertaining space where friends could gather before and after dinner. When I suggested he use this space for his soirées, he expressed doubt about whether a 9-by-12-foot room could entertain anyone. But you know me, I love a challenge.

I also loved the idea that this space could offer intimacy, comfort, and hidden drama—an unexpected surprise for guests. Remember the speakeasies of the 1930s? The secret door would open with a password to reveal a cozy martini lounge. It was pure theater. These off-the-beaten-path rooms can really be fantasy experiences because their design doesn't interrupt the flow of the rest of the house.

To establish this intimate mood, we painted the walls Lowell Lavender, with a semigloss silver shimmer for the trim. Suddenly the room took on a character of its own. A deep color can almost change the dimensions of a small space. The room had several large windows, but very little light actually made it into the room, and the view was not so great. Since we knew the room would primarily be used in the evening, we planned to add mood lighting in Layer Seven, but playing up the shape and architecture of the windows was still important. We chose silver sheer metallic curtains that allowed light to filter in during the day, while obstructing the not-so-great view. By night, however, they added a note of swanky elegance—their soft folds lending a modern shimmer to what was becoming a very retro-inspired space. Still, we needed more detail. We added closet dowels around the ceiling and shirred onto them some deep plum velvet panels. This was the touch that gave the space a luxurious opulence and changed the acoustics entirely. Now every whispered flirtation could be heard.

We loved this fabric so much we kept going, using it to cover a plywood box that reached wall to wall. With a little foam and batting underneath, we created a fabulous banquette that really maximized the seating capacity of the room. Adding a few hinges to the seat also created storage below. Love that!

A few signature pieces of furniture completed the look in Layer Three, starting with a comfortable stamped velvet deco-style club chair in a high-key

magenta. The geometric shape of the chair added a graphic, modern element. Likewise, the faux zebra-skin area rug pulled that graphic underfoot, heightening the drama and enlivening an otherwise dull floor. Can you hear Frankie singing?

Because a party room needs a watering station, we found a wonderful free-standing glass-topped bar. With the addition of a few stools-cum-footrests, we've created seating for almost a dozen people in here. Remember, once an idea hits you, fuel your creative fire with research! Look around for good ideas. Many public gathering areas, for example, especially hotel lobbies and bars, are showcases for beautiful artwork. We took a less expensive approach by adding theatrical black and white photos in matching silver frames to coordinate with the trim. And that clever little ice bucket/table thingie? Well, it could just as easily hold chips or other party favors. I'm thinking martinis shaken, not stirred!

Our homeowner now says this once-useless room is his favorite spot in the house. This is an example of how reclaimed spaces can really inspire you to pursue a dream décor.

Before

TOP What a swinging pad! The lushness of the fabric in this room is key. Velvet sofas and cushy seats make guests feel pampered.

A WORLD OF GLAMOUR IN A SINGLE ROOM ARE YOU NOSTALGIC for days gone by? Do you feel as if your body is here and now, but your soul lives in another era? Well, there's a surefire way to make the past meet the present. Create a fabulous deco-themed room and take a trip back in time.

The roots of this room lie in one of my favorite periods: from the late 1920s to the mid-1930s. You know I love the strong, clean lines and the glamorous details. The deco era is a little bit theatrical, Hollywood inspired, and very chic—everything you need for a legend in the making. The key to re-creating this look is to use rich color, comfortable upholstered seating, and a dash of metallic glitz.

The walls of this room are painted with Peppercorn, a deep green from my paint line. For the lower half of the walls we found some terrific wainscoting. It's just embossed linoleum called Lincrusta, but once installed it looks like either pressed tin or rococo decorative plaster. Here we enhanced the design with a combination of metallic paints. That silver chrome accent was then carried up the walls with strips of metallic tape (from an automotive store— who knew?). Silver-painted wooden appliqué pieces add the final graphic element.

Those fabulous sirens of the silver screen knew that proper placement is everything, so we decided to follow their lead and create a thronelike divan to take center stage in this room. It's actually a twin sleigh bed that serves as a chaise lounge during the day. How's that for a double bill? We raised it up on a platform and, because getting there is half the fun, led up to it with a "premiere" carpet.

Although it may look vintage—and complicated to make—the bed itself is simply an elongated octagonal box made of paintable MDF (Medium Density Fiberboard). The front and back rails have been scooped to create the sleigh effect. If mitered corners are too ambitious for you, you can make the bed a simple rectangle, but we just love this extra detail. Notice how we shaped the side table into the same basic octagon, raised up on a little pedestal.

On both the bed and table, the finish is faux: The intricate inlaid veneer is really just a Hollywood illusion. For

deco living

OPPOSITE Shimmery silver doesn't have to be space age. Look at how these silver-painted chairs add even more glamour to the room. **ABOVE** Floors can add just as much interest and drama to a room as can the walls. This striped floor is a do-it-yourself system available at building supply stores. The graphic bands of alternative color mimic the variety of woods and faux finishes used throughout the room. And to accentuate the height of the chaise lounge, we carried the floor pattern up to the platform with paint.

ABOVE This divan is just divine! All the lines around it are very symmetrical and geometric. That's typical of the deco look.

RIGHT The bed and the vanity are just wooden shapes fitted together like a puzzle. The construction emphasizes two things: strong, clean lines and a stair-step theme. These are what really characterize the furniture and architecture in creating the illusion of the deco period. Cut, print!

During

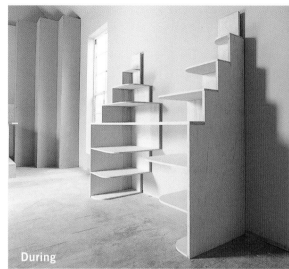

During

the background, we made a comb to "drag" the stain. On top of that we glued tortoiseshell appliqué pieces. The effect is really three-dimensional. Finally, we used simple quarter-round molding to enhance the pedestals and rimmed the base of both pieces with strips of decorative wood molding painted in silver-screen shimmer. Drop-dead gorgeous.

To further emphasize the deco look, we added freestanding columns in each corner of the room. The stair-step outline of these units is a design motif that's very typical of the era, repeated in furnishings and accessories (such as our light sconces, page 63). In addition to subtly changing the architecture of a room, pieces like these can also be fitted for stereo speakers or hinged for additional storage. This stair-step effect in room corners could also be achieved with a folding screen—your choice.

The wonderful lush velvet slipper chair in a shimmery blue-green is a vintage scene-stealer. And what about makeup and wardrobe? We built a vanity using a

ABOVE LEFT Once in a while we like to use a real wood instead of our usual plywood or MDF. Birch was our choice for this vanity, because of its beautiful pale honey color and natural grain. All we needed to do was finish it with a light coat of polyurethane and some pitch-black detailing on the edges. The little stool makes me think of two hatboxes with a mint-green pillbox on top.

ABOVE LEFT AND RIGHT Here's a deco-themed powder room that complements the living room. Notice the strong contrasting colors, the metallic accessories, and the zigzag lines in the mirror and tile work? And those soft vanity lamps! So flattering—at any age!

variation on that same stair-step design. The shelves are actually a series of semi-circular disks slotted into a simple wood frame. With a couple of globe lights and a fabulous mirror, this vanity could make anyone feel like a star.

Lights, camera, action! Wall sconces, hanging ceiling fixtures, and floor lamps all cast a glow in this room. But lighting should be flattering for people and not too bright. Rather, it should create pools of light and shadow. Taking a final inspiration from theatrical costumes, we added a touch of iridescence to the room with striped silk drapes. They pick up the light and create a shimmery effect against the flat-finished walls.

Designing a room like this means you too can be in pictures. Nothing is more satisfying than seeing a dream of cinematic opulence come to life—it's fantasy and escapism at its best. But what really makes this room come together is the backbone of good design and timeless elegance appropriate for any room.

deco sconces
SIMPLE CIRCLES MAKE AN ELEGANT DISPLAY

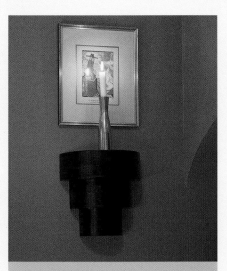

One 4-by-8-foot sheet ¾-inch plywood

1 sheet wiggle board

Wood glue

Finishing nails

Wood screws

Sandpaper

Paint and paintbrush

Hanging screws or picture wire

Table saw

Hammer

Measuring tape and pencil

These sconces can be used as simple display shelves or they can hold candlesticks. In fact, if you make them hollow and leave out the uppermost semicircle, you could outfit the unit with an electric bulb. But if you have a bright bulb or flame close by, it's best to use heat-resistant paint; wood, of course, is flammable. You can find this paint in most hardware or paint stores. If you don't have a table saw, you can use a jigsaw to cut the circles you'll need.

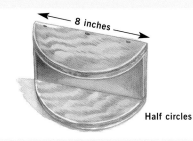

8 inches

Half circles

1. Measure and cut a circle approximately 8 inches in diameter out of ¾-inch plywood. Saw the circle in half along the center. Cut a piece of ¾-inch plywood 8 inches long by 3 inches wide. Attach the 2 half circles to each long edge of the plywood strip using wood glue and finishing nails.

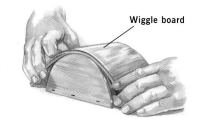

Wiggle board

2. Cut a strip of wiggle board long enough to fit around the edges of the half circle. Glue and nail the wiggle board around the edges.

3. Build the center tier of the sconce the same way as in step 1, increasing the size of the circle by 2 inches. Repeat the construction steps for the top tier of the sconce, making it 2 inches larger than the center tier. Glue and screw the 3 tiers together.

4. Sand and paint or finish as desired. Hang from the wall with screws or picture wire.

coastal living

Sometimes it's a desire to return to nature

that inspires our interiors. But the interpretation of

a natural scene can take many different forms.

Whether you live by the sea or simply want

that feeling in your

home, these makeovers are

sand-washed

for you. (And you're not alone. Some of our

most popular shows by

far are our coastal-living themes.) For

some, *seaside* might mean soft, muted

colors, washed surfaces, and echoes of

marine life. For others it might be a stateroom

aboard a yacht. My "coastal" dream, on page 28,

turned out to have the flavor of a tropical

resort. What's important is to make it *your*

dream, and then make that dream come true.

SOOTHING
SHORES

BAIT & TACKLE

down-by-sea

OPPOSITE When we started, this room was just a bedroom, but now it offers three completely distinct living areas. The multiple-use approach is perfect for guest rooms as well as for studio living (see page 41). In keeping with the beach theme, the four-poster canopy bed was created using natural hemp rope trim, sheer fabric, terry cloth, and mosquito netting—think spa!

FROM THE BEACH TO THE BEDROOM BEFORE WE TURNED this room into a day at the beach, it had a set of French doors and that was about it. There was a plain double bed and a few out-of-scale pieces of furniture that made the space look like a motel room. The room had generous wall space, which would become valuable when transforming it into a charming beachside bungalow.

We began by breaking the space into three distinct areas dictated by function. We needed a sleeping area, a vanity, and a conversation area that would double as a living room. We could play up the bed—already a potential focal point—and we had a long, blank wall that was perfect for the little vanity area. Finally, there was still room for comfortable seating near the doors.

Our dream for this room was of sails billowing in the wind, sand dunes, and warm days on the beach. To help establish this mood, we took the white walls and warmed them up with a soft sand-inspired color trimmed out with cream. We paneled the door with tongue-and-groove boards and gave it a porthole.

Did you know you could build a four-poster canopy bed for about a hundred dollars? That's what we did here. We built our four columns made of a three-tiered assembly of pipe, flanges, and plywood discs. We wrapped Christmas lights around the pipe and stapled pleated sheers over the lights into the discs. At the top and bottom of the column we added some natural hemp rope trim to cover the staples. Now the bed was framed with soft columns of light. For the headboard, we simply covered a piece of ³⁄₄-inch plywood with batting and then with terry cloth. Finally, we draped a store-bought mosquito netting tent over the top, attaching each end to a column. The result is really stunning. Love that bed!

The homeowner had some shells and other beach treasures, but they weren't really grabbing anyone's attention just lying on top of a dresser. Remember, be deliberate when merchandising a room. Shells are just shells, but there's no reason not to give them a seabed of their very own, so we created this shadow box vanity. The construction is simply 2-by-4s with a Plexiglas top and a painted molding surround. We added a gathered skirt for extra concealed storage below. The stool is covered with the same terry-cloth fabric as the bed headboard. When you sit here, it's like going on a mini-vacation.

Natural materials are the key to creating the coastal ambience, so the seating area features wicker chests, sisal rugs, weathered wood, and other *objets trouvé* from flea markets and beachcombing. We sponge-painted old lamps, crackle-finished architectural forms, and hinged together some old shutters to make a folding screen. With a combination of fabulous finds, clever construction, and a lot of imagination, this room has become a coastal hideaway. Go play in the sand!

beachin'

What are some ways to bring the sea right into your cabana?

- Go white. White is the signature shade of the coastal room. You know I'm a fan of color, though, so don't use it as a background color. Try white for the trim and accent colors instead.
- Go natural. Natural fibers and textures are a must in seashore rooms. Use canvas, heavy cotton, wide spa-inspired stripes, terry cloth, and translucent sheers.
- Go organic. Choose organic materials whenever possible. Stone, bamboo, distressed wood, weathered flea-market finds, wicker, reeds, driftwood, grasses, and—of course—shells, shells, shells. (It may seem cliché, but after all, the only place you can find shells is at the beach.) Use them for centerpieces and arrangements, create little still-life vignettes, or use them to dress up plain furniture.

LEFT Talk about cheap chic! The curtain valance over these doors is made out of corrugated cardboard. With some sheer curtains behind, it's a stylish little secret. **ABOVE** The shadow-box vanity is cleverly framed with a tented shape that reminds me of a beach cabana. We attached three flanged pipes to the wall, wrapped them with rope, and glued a starfish on the end of each. Then the valance was simply draped over the top and down both sides.

all
aboard

Before

OPPOSITE Notice how the scale in this room really works well now— the height of the windows is balanced with the height of the bed. But I wouldn't build a headboard like this for anything larger than a double mattress. The result would be a boat bed way too broad across the beam!

FROM SIMPLE TO STATELY THE OWNER OF THIS HOUSE had lived by the ocean for many years. So even when she moved into the landlocked suburbs, she still wanted to retain in her home something of the coastal atmosphere. That's where we came in. We decided to take her guest bedroom—a not-very-seaworthy space with two symmetrical windows and little else—and transform it into a room that was a reflection of her nautical desires.

First of all we had to address Layer One and choose a background color for the walls. A medium cerulean blue was a natural choice. Crisp white was another obvious choice for most of the trim (see "Beachin'," page 69), but we decided to do something a little more interesting for the top of the room. When in bed, of course, you do spend time looking up at the ceiling, especially, say, after a hard day at sea.

At one time or another you may have ripped out some old wood paneling in your home. Pretty useless stuff, right? Wrong! In this room we wanted that "walk-the-plank" look found on ships. So we coated alternating strips of some thin plain wall paneling with three translucent colors to simulate tongue-and-groove boards. After it dried, we secured the paneling to the ceiling. The richness of the wood reflects the light in the room nicely. The cornices over both windows extend right up to the ceiling, making the formerly too-small windows look twice as large. Trimming out the top of the walls with a nautical band of gold molding added a touch of brass sparkle. We also replaced the old ceiling fixture with a genuine porthole light we found at a marine supply store.

At the same store, we found a wealth of objects and icons to further feed our imagination. For instance, we picked up a variety of genuine brass boat fittings to add authenticity to the room. In addition, we found a little rowboat-shaped knickknack shelf that inspired the focal point of the room. What if we could make a headboard in the shape of a boat hull? Well, if you can dream it, you can do it!

When we set to work on the boat bed, we discovered that the tricky part was making sure the face pieces on the sides of the boat curve up toward the bow. To do that, we secured flexible luan to a hull-shaped wooden frame. You can customize this kind of headboard any way you like. We added three fairly deep shelves and screwed brass-painted lights inside them. We lined the hull with bead-board paneling, which further strengthened the shelves and really gave the appearance of ship's planking. Ahoy! We painted the outside face pieces two different colors to represent the waterline, just like on a real boat.

With the bed and the ceiling in place, we already felt like we were in the stateroom of a fabulous cruising yacht. Now all we needed was some storage and

During

ABOVE RIGHT There are plenty of authentic details in this room that help give it that seaside flavor. The prints on the wall, for instance, are real sea charts from the local area, so guests can find their way around! We built the frames out of the same bead-board paneling we used to face the boat bed. **ABOVE** The bed tray and the bookcase are simply altered versions of the side table. You'll find step-by-step instructions on page 73.

display space. For the bedside table and bookshelves, we came up with another nautical-inspired concept. These units are a more elegant version of the old cinder-block-and-plank shelves you had back in your college dorm. The construction is very simple: a series of alternating octagonal towers with pine shelves (see opposite page for step-by-step instructions). What really makes these pieces unique, however, are the rails that run all around the shelves. They're designed to keep your sextant—or, I suppose, your bottle of rum—from sliding off the table when the sea gets choppy. Is that too cool or what?

The bedspread fabric has the jaunty look of a striped awning. When you have a well-established theme like this, you can really have fun with the merchandising of the room. Whether you're combing through marine supply stores and gift shops for those touches of nautica or tide-pooling for starfish and shells, getting there is half the fun!

nautical bedside table

NO-SLIDE SEASIDE SHELVES

Two 4-by-8-foot sheets ¾-inch plywood

Spindle top rails

Wood spindles 2 inches long (part
   #200337 from Van Dyke's Catalog)
   Optional: brass spindles (part
   #02223340) and rails (part
   #02221774 from Van Dyke's
   Catalog)

Wood glue

Wood screws

Finishing nails

Wood stain and brush

Wood putty

Polyurethane

Sandpaper

Power drill

Miter saw

Hammer

These units consist simply of stacked columns and shelves. You can alter the dimensions, making them larger or smaller to fit your space. If the idea of cutting angles puts you off, make the center columns simple squares or rectangles.

1. To make the columns, cut 8 rectangles of wood to desired dimensions (approximately 13 inches high). Miter each of the side edges to a 22.5-degree angle. Fit together into an octagon, securing with wood glue and finishing nails.

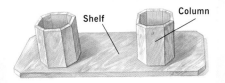

3. To assemble the bookshelves, start with a shelf base and position a column at each end about 6 inches from the outer edges and centered from front to back. Secure from the bottom with glue and wood screws. Continue stacking columns and shelves to the desired height.

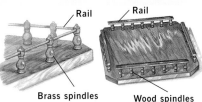

2. To make the shelves, cut 3 squares, slicing off a small triangle at each of the 4 corners to create an octagon shape. You can construct wood rails from scratch or use brass spindles and rails. To make the wood spindles, drill corresponding holes in the holes in the top rail pieces and the shelf; sandwich wood spindles between the 2 pieces. Sand the shelves and seal with polyurethane. When dry, finish with wood stain and polyurethane.

4. To assemble the bedside table, start with a shelf as the base and center a column on top. Glue and screw it in place from the bottom. Stack octagons and shelves, positioning the columns in the center of the shelves and nail or screw through the shelf into the top edges of the column.

sanctuary by the shore

HARMONY EN SUITE YOU'VE HEARD ME SAY it a million times: Your master bedroom suite deserves to be a pampering space. This is where you begin and end each day; it's your retreat from the rest of the world. So when you move into a house or you're remodeling a home, tackle this room project first.

It's also important to create a relationship between the master bedroom and the master bathroom. We often think we can treat these two spaces differently just because we can close the door. Not so. Most likely you've got the door to the bath open as much as you've got it closed. The first and easiest way to begin the relationship is with color.

In this master suite, the builder had already linked the two rooms by using the same sandstone tile on the fireplace in the bedroom and in the bathroom shower and vanity areas. We painted the bedroom walls a lovely deep tan color to go with the tile and used dove gray on the ceiling. Because the room was such a tall space, over 9 feet, we chose a darker color for the ceiling to bring it down a little bit and make the room feel more intimate. We reversed the colors in the master bathroom, using dove gray as the wall color and tan as the ceiling color. The wall/ceiling switch is a terrific idea to visually connect two adjoining rooms.

Our next task was to add some architectural elements to the relatively featureless bedroom. Windows on each side of the fireplace were long and narrow with alcove arches above. We ordered arched pediments from a mail-order catalog, placed them above the windows, and painted them the same color as the trim. Below, wooden blinds that matched the baseboard trim were added for privacy, and generous fabric panels were draped from a pole. On the adjacent wall, windows overlooking a small garden area were capped with a single cornice, nice thick crown molding, and a deep reveal. Underneath, in identical fabric, drapes were hung to swoop back over the blinds and the sliding glass door behind them.

The placement of the king-size bed in the room was tricky. It seemed to block a doorway or window in every direction. The only solution was to place it on a diagonal in the center of the room, angled toward the fireplace. We then had a spot for the matching dresser behind the headboard and we anchored this slumber "island" with two matching bed stands.

Because the space is taller than it is wide, we worked to find ways to furnish the areas overhead, but we were careful to follow our monochromatic color scheme. To widen the room, we detached the mirror from the dresser and hung

Before

OPPOSITE We dressed up the bed with a beautiful damask beige comforter to conform to our monochromatic color scheme. The neutral tone-on-tone minimizes the size of the bed and also provides a solution to a common problem: finding fabrics that make both spouses happy. This one is tailored enough for him, yet luxurious enough for her.

Before

it over the mantel. Not only does it reflect all of our handiwork, but it also continues the arch shape we established in the window treatments.

We brought the same ideas we used in the master bedroom into the bathroom to transform it into a luxurious spa. We created a focal point around the tub by hanging a Roman shade from the ceiling over the window above it. On the adjoining wall we suspended a single ocean-inspired oil painting teamed with a decorative bracketed shelf below. Scented candles and tropical plants made this functional place into a seductive environment.

When we organized the daily essentials into wire baskets on the vanity, the chrome became the jewelry of the room. In our lighting layer, two lamps for the vanity help add romance. In the evening, harsh overheads can be turned off,

ABOVE RIGHT Even with the basics in place, our room theme still called for accessories. So we suspended two floral prints from wire attached to the ceiling. Using hot glue and two lengths of white ribbon, we covered the wire. The illusion is that the ribbon is the hanging device. Sneaky but effective, don't you think?

allowing the flicker of candlelight to add serenity during a soak in the tub. A large floral arrangement placed on the vanity provides scale and adds color, fragrance, and life to the space. Luckily, there was just enough room to add a bamboo bench along the wall by the shower—an organic element that provides a place of repose. I love a place to sit down in the bathroom, don't you?

I think this bedroom is one of our best ever: We took a rather charmless space with a tricky floor plan, a great big bed, a narrow pass-through bathroom and—with some thought to the mood we wanted to create—brought to life a real coastal retreat. Sweet dreams!

LEFT Underneath each window, we built simple plywood boxes for storage of out-of-season clothing and bedding. With the addition of upholstered cushions and piles of throw pillows, the storage boxes have become fabulous window seats. The drapes, swept to the side and tied back, just barely touch the top of the seats.

ABOVE The surfaces on top of the armoire and the tables were opportunities for great still-life vignettes. A shell-encrusted lamp and distressed whitewashed accessories add a seaside feeling with chic country flair.

BRINGING SERENITY TO THE SHORE I DON'T need to tell you that I have a fondness for the tropics. You can see this in the bedroom on the opposite page. And you might be interested to know that our show was the first to focus on spiritual, Zen-inspired places. Your response to these kinds of interiors has kept us continually refining that look and developing new ways to integrate it into room redos. After all, there's a reason why import stores have proliferated in the last few years. They sell products that provide a global connection and bring to mind a sense of mystery, serenity, and tranquillity.

When I entered this homeowner's house, the first things that caught my eye were the ancient tribal masks and other interesting objects she had collected from around the world. But these items looked a bit out of place. After a long chat, she told me of her love of travel, and how she wanted her bedroom to make her feel as if she were on vacation. She had never pursued that dream, however, because she felt it would be beyond her budget. That's just the kind of challenge we love.

The bedroom was fairly charmless; it contained two undersize, narrow windows on one wall. The ceiling was low and there were doors to the bathroom and hallway that left only one place for the bed to go. Even though the room was small, we wanted to play up rather than minimize the bed. But given the size of the bed and the fact that the room was already dark, we realized we'd have to bring some extra man-made light into the room. That meant we didn't have to worry about the effect of daylight on our wall colors. We wanted a monochromatic palette, and chose a deep khaki taupe for the walls and a rich linen color for the trim.

The windows were our main concern. If we built them up too much, the room would look unbalanced. But at the same time, we wanted to infuse the room with a sense of old-world architecture. Then it hit us—why not add two more windows to the wall behind the bed? We'd have to think of a way to create these false windows on a small budget. The trick was to use the same treatment for the two real and the two false windows. We made arched wooden cornices that could house both a pull-down shade and curtains. On the real windows we extended the cornices 8 inches past the casings to give the appearance that the windows were wider than they really are. For the false windows, we took inexpensive mirror tiles and stuck them to the wall in the same shape as the real windows. Once the import shades were installed, you could just see a flicker of light through the bamboo slats of the blinds. Is that clever or what?

The hardwood floors were not in great shape, but we knew that between the

south sea haven

Before

OPPOSITE With the addition of a frame, the bed looked like a wrought-iron four-poster. We hung our fabric panels and chose bed linens and a comforter called Zensational (see "Resources"). We deliberately kept the palette more toward textures than patterns. Suddenly, we had an amazing bed.

bed and an area rug, very little of the floor would show. So we gave the floors a good cleaning. Now the shell of the room was complete except for the ceiling. It took some pondering, but one evening I found a photo of a Balinese hotel room. The room's ceiling was thatched with what appeared to be a natural fiber held in place with dark beams. The lightbulb went off in my head.

We used the same inexpensive bamboo shades that looked so good on the windows. We removed the hardware, stapled them to the ceiling, and used 1-by-3-

ABOVE LEFT If you're covering a ceiling with material, mark out a diagram on paper with accurate measurements. Generally, if there is a light fixture, you will probably want a wooden strip on either side, the strip butting the mounting.
ABOVE CENTER It's all about scale. This ladder shelf is exactly the right size to balance out the windows, and it's substantial enough to hold weighty accessories.
ABOVE RIGHT Careful arrangement creates still-life vignettes.
OPPOSITE We used deep orange as a complementary accent color throughout the space.

inch pine strips coated with walnut stain to simulate beams. But before we did the entire ceiling with this treatment, we first made a sample panel of the treatment on plywood. When we held it up to the ceiling, we fell in love!

Now the bed itself seemed to call for exotic netting to give it that tropical feeling. But the existing headboard provided no point of attachment for billowing sheers. So off we went to the plumbing section of our hardware store! All it took was several lengths of PVC piping, six plastic PVC elbows, and several "T" connectors of the same material. We were able to put together a freestanding frame that sat on the floor. Because we planned to hang only light fabric from this frame, it didn't need to be any more complicated or heavy than that. To paint the PVC, we first coated it with a base of Kilz, a primer for nonporous surfaces, and then sponge-painted it with the same stain we used for the ceiling.

Around the room, inexpensive import pieces resembled artifacts from globe-trotting adventures. To illuminate the space, we placed uplights under potted palms, and votive candles and Asian-inspired lamps on table surfaces.

Inspired by what seemed to be an unattainable dream, this room is proof that with enthusiasm and problem solving, you can overcome any obstacles. It's not about the money; it's about having the courage to follow your heart.

breaking spaces

You've heard me talk about "breaking spaces" in rooms. Well this house really exemplifies this technique. The whole house seemed to revolve around a giant atrium, and many of the rooms were connected by arched openings

spacious

FAMILY

rather than doors. There

were views in every

direction. But the

owners wanted to make it a

comfortable family

home. Take a look at

how we handled these

awkward spaces.

welcoming

open

foyer eyes only

MAKING AN ENTRANCE GRAND NOW JUST BECAUSE this entrance looks grand, think that it has nothing to offer an ordinary citizen. If you look closely at the floor plan, this pass-through space is not very large, measuring a scant 8 by 10 feet. However, it is undeniably tall, so anything in it is simply dwarfed. I call these kinds of rooms "come-on spaces" because builders know they appeal to people's egos. Imagine the scene: The potential homeowner enters, gives a gasp of delight, and says, "I'm rich! Won't the neighbors be jealous?" Only after they move in do the inhabitants realize that the grand entrance has robbed space from all the other rooms in the house. So they've simply paid through the nose for an entry while the guest bedroom is the size of a postage stamp. At two and half stories high, it's intimidating. So how do you bring intimacy to a space like this while adding function?

Faced with this prospect, we didn't have a collective heart attack. Instead, we decided to paint. We chose a deep warm golden color called Pumpkin Pie. To defray the costs, we left the trim and the stair balusters white, as we did elsewhere in the house. The crisp trim against the deep yellow gold would also help soak up the light streaming in from the floor-to-ceiling windows. To make the ceiling appear a bit lower, we painted it a putty color called Cream of Mushroom. Even without any other layers, the space already went from mausoleum to museum. So far, so good.

The floor and stairs were natural wood and marble, so we had to deaden the sound. We started by adding a few upholstered side chairs, which also added texture, and found more opportunities to use fabric in the window treatment. We attached simple closet doweling with wood finials onto inexpensive wood brackets just below the ceiling line between each window combination and on each side of the front door. We hung panels of sheer white fabric all the way from the ceiling to the floor. Can you imagine opening the door and being greeted by columns of cascading fabric?

To absorb even more sound we put a nice little area rug in the center of the foyer, which also helps to define the space. Now it was time to turn our attention to function. Against one wall we placed a crackle-finish chest, providing handy linen storage close to the laundry room. We put a center table on the area rug; it would be a place to hold mail, car keys, garage-door openers, and whatnot. Finally, we set a small credenza in the curve of the stairwell. This would be an ideal place to store entertaining extras, such as candles, spare napkins and coasters, and party favors.

Before

Adding to the scale of the furnishings were two old-world ceramic pedestals stacked on top of one another. A matching urn was placed on each pedestal—one to the left of the front door and the other opposite the stairwell landing. Now it was time to add the all-important final layer of plants and lighting. Atop the pedestals we added Kentia palms that reach for the ceiling. The umbrella of palm fronds overhead created another lowering devise. At night, with uplights, shadows danced from the plants for a wonderful effect of intimacy. Taking our cue from public hotel lobbies, we added a floral focal point to the center table. We added tall identical lamps to the white chest to illuminate the poster and add a cozy glow to that side of the space.

So what was once a cold, space-robbing foyer had turned into a viable, practical living space. From the time guests first enter the home they are treated to a preview of what to expect in the rest of the house. The next time height intimidates you, think tall!

ABOVE LEFT Furnish entries in a home as living spaces with seating and storage. The overscale reproduction poster creates a focal point that balances the size and height of the staircase.

ABOVE The window-over-window combinations of this grand two-story foyer are challenging when it comes to window treatments. Should they be treated separately or together? And look at those white walls! Columns of white fabric cascading from ceiling to floor unite the windows without blocking the light.

MOVING COAST TO COAST I'VE READ THAT only about 20 percent of Americans have the chance to decorate their homes from scratch more than once in a lifetime. For the most part, we're forced to work with the space and ambience of a home we acquire. That was the case with the couple who occupy this home. They had lived in Ohio until they relocated to Southern California. And that meant we were faced with several dilemmas.

Moving can be a strain all by itself, but suppose you buy a house that has a whole different design sensibility from your previous residence? This couple moved from a more traditional neighborhood to one that was trendy and funky. The other problem was that their first home was a series of very defined rooms. Here, the open floor plan meant that the contents of each room would be visible from many vantage points. Our challenge was to tie the whole scheme together.

One of the easiest ways to do this was to develop a great paint palette for every room of the house. But in an open floor plan like this, where do you stop and start your paint colors? First of all, we decided to keep the existing white trim and natural wood baseboards. Not only did that minimize paint costs, but it made sense for a seaside community (see "Beachin'" on page 69 for more coastal decorating tips). We then chose an additional four colors to mix and match throughout the space. Remember, the colors had to be compatible. Because of the visibility of one room from another, the flow of color needed to enhance the space rather than chop it up.

Because the trim and the baseboards would be consistent, we felt that the ceiling color should follow suit. This would help with the overhead flow. So all the ceilings became a deep taupe color called Cream of Mushroom from my paint line. Then, for the walls, we chose the following: a dusty sage green; a warm, rich color called Pumpkin Pie; and a complementary deep putty. Why didn't they clash? Well, what makes it all work is choosing colors that have the same hue value. The intensity or saturation of the color is at the same level whether it's gold or green. For practical purposes, this means all the colors fall in the same position on the paint color strips. We didn't build in accent color at this stage, but saved it for later layers with our fabric and accessories.

If you use the instincts you already have, breaking color from room to room doesn't have to be a difficult task. It's just like applying makeup. Think of foundation as being a wall color and your eye shadow and lip color as being the acces-

wide-open spaces

OPPOSITE This is the entrance to the living room—a huge archway that overlooks the foyer and meant very little privacy for those inside. We flanked it with rich opulent drapes shirred onto a pole at the ceiling and tied back to the wall. The drapes soften the edges of the entry and warm up the living space.

sories and accents. But remember to disperse the color evenly throughout all visible spaces. And keep in mind that the foundation is just Layer One. By the time you add six more layers to the room, it simply becomes background.

Fortunately, much of the furniture the homeowners brought with them from their previous home was natural and timeless, which made integrating it much easier. (The florals stayed behind!) The upholstered pieces were primarily in textures and solids, so we were able to mix and match the furniture throughout the space, just as we did the wall colors. For instance, they had two rust-colored sofas that were originally placed in one room. We separated them into two adjoining spaces so both rooms had the influence of that color. But even the open space needed a little warmth and luxury.

This is really when Layer Four, Accent Fabrics, can come to the rescue. We introduced simple, generous fabric panels at key areas in the upper floor. We added one pair of velvet drapes to the entertainment room, but rather than keeping them close to the window frames, we took the fabric all the way over to the walls and pulled them away from the window with tiebacks. This helps to deaden the acoustics from the adjoining two-story foyer and soak up the TV sounds as well.

We filled a transplanted whitewashed armoire and bookcase wall unit with books and accessories. Although it seemed like a lot of whitewash against the pumpkin-colored walls, it was less stark once the accessories were added. A large Boston fern on top brings the eye up to artwork above.

Just a reminder: A lot of your accessories may need upgrading or simply be out of proportion to their new setting. Consider passing them on to someone else to enjoy and choose new objects that look a little more deliberate. My rule of thumb is to have fewer big pieces and less room "dandruff"—you know, those things that clutter surfaces and rob you of valuable living space. By utilizing the classic furniture pieces you have, you'll save money to spend on the extras.

The large living room was the trickiest room in the house. It opens up into the breakfast nook and kitchen. This is a mingling and gathering place, so it needed to be comfortable and intimate. Again, we used furnishings and fabric. Matching drapes were tied back on each window surrounding the fireplace, then reinterpreted in the custom Roman shades in the breakfast area. In the absence of dividing walls, it is up to the furniture to define specific conversation areas. We finished off the room with some tall Kentia palms on pedestals with uplights, and with task and accent lighting.

OPPOSITE AND BELOW RIGHT
The furniture creates different environments in the same space. We placed a leather sofa at right angles to the fireplace. Two club chairs near the railing make a nice conversation area. The chenille settee is a cross-linking device between the two areas. The green chairs against the yellow backdrop of the foyer cross-pollinates the green from the dining room. Two ottomans complete the seating arrangement and still allow 18 inches to pass between pieces. A coffee table with welcome storage is perfectly in scale. And a screen with a mirror behind it provides the illusion of light behind.

Before

ABOVE We replaced an underscale glass table in the breakfast nook with a more substantial round glass table and fully upholstered chairs. The chairs echo the green of the living room club chairs, again creating continuity and pulling the eye from room to room. Yes, the eye always goes to color.

RIGHT A large-screen TV, which doesn't look good on any coast, was positioned in the entertainment room opposite the windows, so it could be seen only from within that room. To further minimize the TV, we put a tchotchke on top and backlit it to distract the eye to the pictures on the wall behind it.

easy ottoman

PUT YOUR FEET UP

We came up with a fun, "low"-sew solution for this multipurpose piece of furniture. It's a slipcover ottoman that requires almost no stitching, but the frame is sturdy enough to hold a tray of tea and biscuits. Small pieces of furniture such as this can be reupholstered easily to suit your décor when you decide to change it.

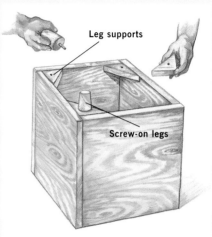

Leg supports

Screw-on legs

2. Cut 4 triangles from ¾-inch plywood to support the legs. Attach them to each corner of the bottom of the ottoman, nailing from the outside edges. Predrill the holes, then screw the legs into each triangular support.

One 4-by-8-foot sheet ¾-inch plywood

4 wood legs with screw-in ends

1½-inch upholstery foam to cover sides and top

Upholstery fabric (1½ yards by 54 inches)

Finishing nails

Screws

Nails

Spray adhesive

Scissors or rotary cutter and mat

Sewing machine, thread, and pins

Staple gun and staples

Hammer

Power drill

Power saw

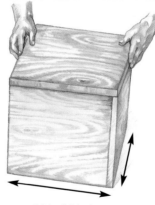

16 by 16 inches

1. Cut 5 squares of ¾-inch plywood of equal dimensions and fasten together with finishing nails to form 4 sides and a top. We made ours 16 inches square.

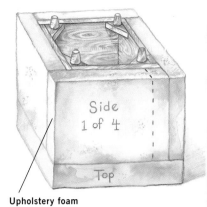

Upholstery foam

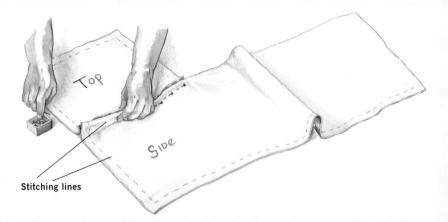

Stitching lines

3. Cut 5 pieces of 1½-inch upholstery foam and glue to plywood sides and top using spray adhesive. Overlap the side pieces by 1½ inches, the thickness of the foam. Cut the top foam piece 3 inches larger than the top plywood piece.

4. Cut upholstery fabric equal to the perimeter of the foam-covered ottoman (the width of all 4 sides added together, plus 1 inch for the seam allowance) by the height of the ottoman plus 4 inches. Cut a square of upholstery fabric 1 inch larger than the measurements of the top including the foam. With right sides together, pin the side strip to the top square, pivoting the fabric at each corner. Place pins perpendicular to the stitching line so the sewing machine can stitch over them. Stitch around the top square using a ½-inch seam allowance. Stitch the side strip closed.

5. Turn the slipcover right side out and slip it over the ottoman. Pull the excess fabric under the bottom and staple to the plywood underneath.

Staple under here

Upholstery foam

retro rooms

Every now and then I just like to let

loose my imagination and design rooms

that are fun, bold, and zany. Decorating a room like

this might seem over the top, but it's a great way to

express yourself and create a space that makes

FUN

JAZZ

eclectic color

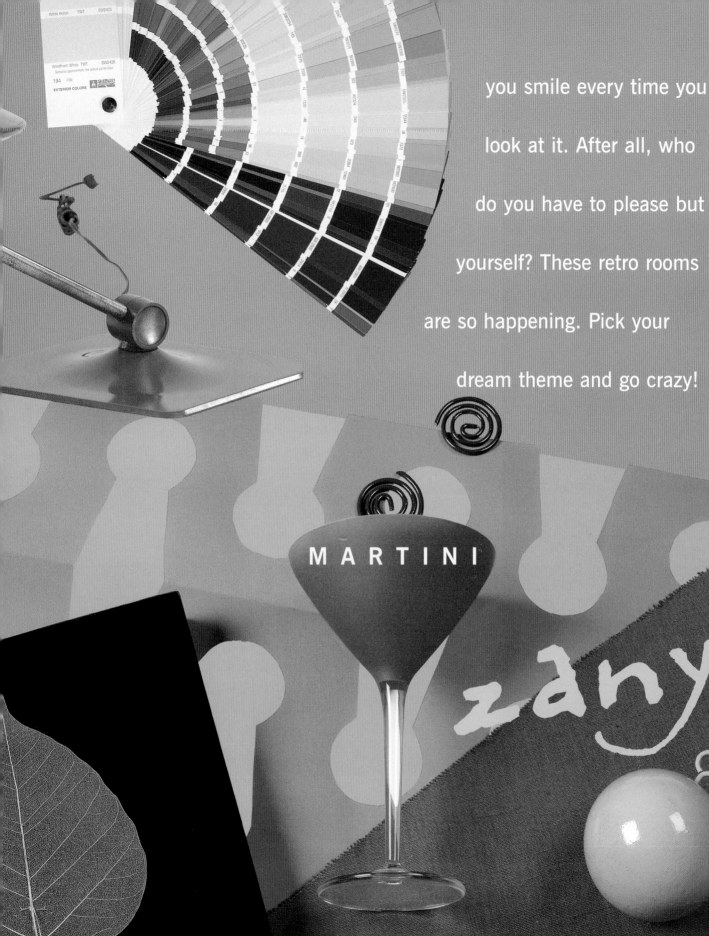

you smile every time you look at it. After all, who do you have to please but yourself? These retro rooms are so happening. Pick your dream theme and go crazy!

MARTINI

zany

pop
tartz

DYNAMIC DÉCOR ON A BUDGET WHAT HAPPENS WHEN you pair some fabulous modern furniture with lots of bold shapes and colors? You get a very dynamic room, indeed. Groovy, baby!

In fact, it was the furniture that was the spark for this room's theme. Designed by Harry Siegal, it's a mixture of almost cartoonlike chairs and tables that are surprisingly comfortable, imaginative, and effective. One of the more eye-catching pieces is a multicolored one-armed couch. A circular upholstered coffee table is another attention getter. And how do you like that easy chair covered in faux fur? Today's technology reinterprets the past.

We knew right off the bat that we were going to use a lot of color in this room, so we wanted a wall treatment that could hold its own as a backdrop for the furniture. The end result is a great example of how you can use an ordinary material to create a really extraordinary effect. We took shiny corrugated aluminum panels and used them horizontally as wainscoting. We simply attached them to the wall with self-tapping aluminum screws. But a word of warning if you want to try this look. Aluminum edges are sharp! Wear gloves and handle with care. I guess interior decorating can be dangerous.

For the upper part of the walls, we went in the opposite direction and marked off alternating wide stripes of glossy black on white. The combination of vertical and horizontal visually raises the roof. Near the top of each white stripe we placed a glossy black wooden block with a hot-glued leaf print. The effect is high tech but organic. Totally hip.

Before

During

OPPOSITE We bought nylon storage bags from Ikea and strung them onto Christmas lights for a column of illumination in one corner.

LEFT I love the various colors mixed and matched on this furniture. Yet the styles are very classic. If you ever want to reupholster in a more neutral shade (following my advice, of course), then you can. Notice how the triangular panels echo the panels on the coffee table/ottoman. Zebra stripes and faux fur are a must in a retro room.

The floor treatment is similarly psychedelic but a little less attention-grabbing. Remember good old-fashioned linoleum? It's pretty easy to find remnant pieces at home stores. We bought a few and cut them into really cool irregular shapes to liven up a fairly dull floor. Amoeba area rugs!

Here's a fun project for a rainy day when school's out: paper dolls for grown-ups! The "curtain" is actually made out of two layers of tissue paper from the art-supply store. The first layer is made of cutouts just like those snowflakes you make at Christmastime. The second tissue layer is a series of repeating geometric triangles. The double layer filters the daylight but still keeps the room bright so you get the full effect of all these vibrant colors and shapes.

There are plenty of other eye-catching accessories on display here. That stair-step rolling cabinet in the corner was another do-it-yourself project made of storage boxes (see opposite for step-by-step instructions). And we made a shaggy light shade by turning a regular shade upside down and gluing overlapping ribbons to it. How much does *that* cost? Less than the price of a milk shake in 1959!

There's a lot going on in the room, but that's what it's all about—lots of color and a sense of humor. It's hip, it's happening, it's you, baby!

ABOVE RIGHT What would a party room be like without a bar? There's almost always a corner to squeeze one in. Note the ribbon lamp shade just to the left of it.

"mod"ular shelves
STORAGE, ROLLED AND STACKED

Our retro-inspired "mod"ular shelves are so happening. I love this unit's mobility—it could work anywhere in the house. Each cube is perfect to display a single accessory. Either purchase store-bought cubes or make simple boxes from plywood. Add more cubes, build a tower in the center, and use it as a room divider. When your needs change, add shelves and make bookcases. They're so simple, so chic, and so cool.

5 or more purchased wooden storage
    cubes (ours came from Ikea)

8 casters

Wood putty

Sandpaper

Painter's tape

Primer

Latex enamel in colors of choice (we
    used bright gold, blue, and orange)

Wood screws

Wood glue

Power drill and screwdriver

Paintbrushes

Roller and tray

1. Assemble the storage cubes according to the manufacturer's directions, leaving out the interior shelves. Decide on the configuration design by laying the cubes out on the floor facing upward so gravity works for you. Each unit must have 2 end cubes of equal height and a span of no more than 4 or 5 cubes.

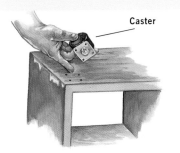

Caster

3. Predrill holes in the sides of each cube and then secure the cubes together in the desired configuration with wood screws and wood glue.

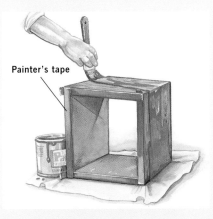

Painter's tape

2. Fill in all interior shelf peg holes with wood putty and let dry. Sand each of the cubes, then prime all surfaces and let dry. Paint the tops, sides, and insides of each cube different colors. To paint, first cover the top, sides, and inside edges using painter's tape. Then prime and paint all the edges a single color and let dry. Remove the tape and apply tape to the front edges, then prime and paint the remaining surfaces.

4. Attach a caster to the bottom of each of the 4 corners of the 2 end cubes. Locking casters will keep the unit from rolling away.

retro chic

COLOR INSPIRES A BLAST TO THE PAST WE'VE SEEN RETRO-themed rooms that reflect a single time period, but you don't need to be historically correct to create a lavish interior that gives you the feel and flavor of another era. This room uses bright colors as a starting point to bring together elements of the 1930s, '40s, '50s, '60s, and even '70s.

I know some of you are hesitant to express yourself with color. But remember, where there is fear there is no creativity. That's why I asked you in our Dream Questionnaire back on page 23 to think of a color without reference to anything else—not a particular set of walls, piece of furniture, article of clothing, or piece of pottery! You never know where that color might take you. In this room we picked the color chartreuse. And that's what we started with when we set out to revamp this nondescript living room. Would you believe it's the same room as our "Four Rooms in One," shown on page 41.

The particular paint shade we used for the wall was Summer Savory from the Christopher Lowell Paint Collection. It's a dusty shade that's soft enough to create a dramatic background without overwhelming the room; true chartreuse was added as an accent color. You know I don't like to see bedsheet-white ceilings, so we did the ceiling in a cooler shade called Bay Leaf Blush. The trim is called Sea Salt.

Once you choose a strong color scheme like this, it gives you the freedom to revel in further possibilities. It's as if you've already stuck your neck out, so you might as well go for broke. And by establishing this hip look here in Layer One, we felt free to jazz up the room using even more snazzy retro-inspired colors. Love that! Visions of everything from Andy Warhol posters to fuzzy dice dangling from rearview mirrors danced in our heads.

Drapes in a deep eggplant color match accents on the wall. Below the window seat, we added a row of purple Tupperware lids for a touch of geometric whimsy. We made a slanted-back chair of painted plywood and upholstered it in a plum-colored retro print fabric. That deep glossy paint on the coffee table is a really cool neon blue Hammerite paint. This paint is amazing. After it dries, it looks like hammered metal. That, combined with colored aluminum pipe, becomes a groovy but practical workhorse for the room.

Remember those linoleum floors that went away in the 1950s? A remnant of this humble material, cut into a rug, is another geometric accent that pulls pattern down to the not-so-hot floor.

A standout in the room is the honey-colored leather sofa that just screams "deluxe." It's a style and color that straddles several eras and truly fits the defi-

nition of "timeless." After all, if you're going to spend money on a leather sofa, better make sure it will stand the test of time! We also made a "deco" stair-step table out of four stacked plywood boxes mounted to each other with "L" brackets—no kidding. What's great about this table is the flexibility you have in positioning it. You can adjust all the tiers so they're flush on one side. This really works well when you place it against a wall. Or you can center all the tiers so that there is equal space all the way around if you wish to use it as a centerpiece. Add a light inside for a floating effect.

Dispersing bold color evenly around the room helps unify the space by giving it balance. One of the things that ties the room together is a dowel screen that matches the coffee table. We found these anodized aluminum pipes at a metal supply store and set them into wooden frames. When assembled, each panel picks up a different color used in the room. In the end, although this room is chock-full of extraordinary ideas, it's the uninhibited sense of play and cheerful attitude that make it work.

ABOVE We spread out the wealth of color in this room so that no one shade dominates. This allows the eye to absorb the whole room as a balanced space and maintains a harmony between the furniture and the accessories. If you place too many objects of similar color together, they will throw the room off-balance. Here again, think of your wardrobe when dispersing color. Choose a basic color scheme and dress it up with accents. Note how great our new uncovered window looks.

the hardworking home

When you think of corporate office reception areas,

or work areas in general, the key words that might

come to mind are *serious, utilitarian,* or even *cold*

and intimidating. Well, in my own offices I was

faced with the challenge of creating a gracious,

inviting atmosphere that would not only welcome

clients from all over the world but would also be

inspiring to my wonderful working family. We

wanted to make an environment that could

DUAL-FUNCTION

productive

flexible

GLOBAL DESIGN

accommodate

a lot of activity and also bring global design

influence into the workplace. So we used lots of

decorating tricks to create spaces that

encourage productivity *and*

creativity.

belly up to the bar

A RECEPTION ROOM THAT SAYS "WELCOME" SHOULD A reception desk make you think of security, appointments, and phones ringing off the hook? Well, we didn't want that. Instead, we dreamed of a setting that would promote good feelings from the moment you walked in the front door. On a recent trip to Hawaii I had enjoyed having drinks at a great little beverage hut on the beach. I thought, why not bring that same feeling of camaraderie into the reception area? So we duplicated the bar from one of these huts, turning a necessary functional element into this way-cool natural gathering place. Don't you see yourself saying, "I'll have another one of those tropical drinks and don't forget the umbrella!"

The construction of the bar/reception desk may look complicated, but it's simply a plywood base with a top shaped like a boomerang. We covered the sides with half-rounds of mail-order 4-inch bamboo glazed to coordinate with the wood in the room. Flexible molding surrounds the top, nd with strategically

During

placed bumps of hot glue and paint, it's been made to look like bamboo to match the sides. We finished the top surface with gold-leafing paper over a terra-cotta-colored base coat and applied lots and lots of polyurethane to make it really durable. It turned out so well we decided to incorporate the exotic theme throughout the room and into other spaces in our office.

We used the same bamboo half-rounds as a wainscoting on the wall, attached to caning-covered luan (thin wood veneer). This created a wainscoting that visually united each wall. Below, faux bamboo caps it off. This treatment helped to visually unite each wall. Faux bamboo (made by applying hot-glue bumps to a wood half-round) is such a cool idea. Think how terrific this could be in your dining room or foyer.

When we inherited the office, the entrance doors were an eyesore—painted brown with ugly hardware. Here again, we covered thin luan with woven sea grass material edged with gold-colored trim to create removable panels. These helped carry on the nature theme. There are surely surfaces in your home that could benefit from this disguising treatment.

What about paint? Each wall received a different but compatible hue, from Lowell Lavender to Brined Grape Leaves to Burned Butter and Clay Cotta. We

OPPOSITE Could we have a home-away-from-home that looked professional? By disguising the functional elements and adding lots of warm materials and colors, we turned this reception area into a warm and inviting space.

painted the suspended ceiling panels Light Lowell Lavender. For those of you who think that painting the ceiling dark is going to make the room look closed in, check it out. Gold-painted crown molding separates the wall and ceiling colors while adding accent sparkle to draw the eye upward.

The focal point of the reception room was the upholstered wall opposite the entry door. The fabric is a warm gold chenille with a visible grain. Our friend Thomas Gill cut out and stitched together large squares of the fabric, shifting the grain to create a diamond pattern. He stapled padding to the wall and then sta-

pled the stitched fabric panel over it. This single upholstered wall serves a host of functions: It changes the acoustics in the room, adds layered texture, and makes the space more opulent—an unexpected touch in an office.

To add privacy and soften the view down a long hall, we attached a pole and luscious plum velvet drape to the ceiling. We then pulled back the drape with a luxurious tassel tieback. More fabric dressed the upholstered furniture pieces. A console with an Asian flair suits any environment. Here it holds a lamp on top and a couple of prints with characters depicting "good health," "good luck," and "prosperity"—all positive thoughts for any worker or things business.

For storage, we translated the Asian look into a freestanding tonsu-inspired stair-step cubbie. It also serves as a divider between the reception area and the back hallway. We trimmed out the tonsu with faux bamboo to tie it into the reception desk. When we put this together, I immediately thought what a great dividing element it would make in a living room.

Any room in your home that needs help can benefit from the global design influence of this gracious and inviting décor. Rich color, bamboo, silk here and there, plus the use of organic elements can accomplish that worldly look.

OPPOSITE AND ABOVE A warm and exotic juxtaposition of colors, fabric textures, and organic materials is illustrated in these vignettes. The stair-step tonsu is dressed up with a variety of artifacts that provide decorative storage and make a great statement.

ONE HOME OFFICE, FOUR WAYS THINK ABOUT A LARGE open area like a remodeled basement or a finished garage. How often do we really use those big empty spaces? Why not take some tips from my office where several employees share one room, creating what we call "pods"—rooms within a room. The idea here is uniform individuality—everybody gets a similar station of his or her own. Or if necessary, the space can shift and change to accommodate the family's needs.

In this new century, things are whizzing by so fast that we can barely keep up. Our living spaces must be flexible enough to respond to those changes. Like it or not, everyone eventually is going to be online. And each family member wants to use the home office for something different. Dad wants to book airline tickets. Sis wants to catch up on the hottest boy band. Mom wants a quiet space to do some research. Each member wants her own private "place" to work.

So how do we keep everybody happy? Well, in this open space we created four separate, secluded workstations by sectioning off a great big square set diagonally in the center of the room. We positioned tall computer armoire towers facing each corner and lined the back of them with bookcases facing into this common center square. Each person has his or her own specific work area, and no station is visible to the center space or any other space in the room. We think that is sensational.

Just about any office supply center, superstore, or catalog sells a version of a computer armoire—whether it's in white melamine or a wood tone. Remember, you'll need to put these together, and after you've assembled them (about, oh, a year and half later), paint them, give them a faux finish, or just leave them the way they are.

These more expensive armoires look great from the front but with their unfinished backs, they aren't made to stand free-floating in the center of a room. We got around this by backing bookcases up to them. From the doorway, there is a dramatic room-within-a-room view. We have just enough room in the center for a table and four fabulous chairs—a common library area where the family can mingle and discuss ideas, or work on joint projects.

We left the areas between the workstations open in order to be able to maneuver easily from one to another. This also

family
online

OPPOSITE Just to prove you don't have to sacrifice design for function, we created this beautiful library by backing bookcases up against four computer armoire workstations. Adding books and eye-catching accessories makes the cozy interior space feel homey.

gave us great opportunities to add fabric. We had aluminum pipes custom-bent and flanged to connect each station with drapery panels. The drapes added a homey atmosphere when we tied them back with wonderful tassels. Closing the drapes ensures that conversation in the library isn't interrupting anyone who is hard at work elsewhere.

Lighting is also important. In the library we used utilitarian clip-on lights that have three settings of brightness for maximum flexibility. When the lights are on their dim setting, it's very moody. And when they're up full, you can see very clearly to read.

Each family member can design his or her own workstation. One of our four stations has a wonderful crackle-finished screen and a beautiful bamboo plant. Uplights? Absolutely. Moving over to another corner reveals a couple of nice club chairs and a sideboard. That's great. The next pod is more of a unisex habitat with Asian-inspired artwork. As always, the key is to use your imagination and incorporate the things you love into your work environment.

Open spaces can be completely transformed by using rich color. Dare to use different colors on each wall, but keep them all in the same hue value. Remember that after you've added great furniture, accessories, and fabric, the wall color simply becomes background. So don't let technology intimidate or ruin the decor. What you hate, decorate!

ABOVE LEFT More matching bookcases like the ones in the library unite the two spaces while offering more opportunities for accessorizing. A crackle-finish pedestal adds charm, and fabric panels in three coordinating prints fill the wall.

ABOVE RIGHT This space is defined by a buttery yellow wall and minimal accessories. The bamboo plant is lit from below, casting feathery shadows on a crackle-finish screen.

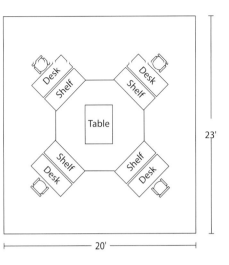

23'

20'

ABOVE Elevation of the work station room.

LEFT A collection of four Japanese prints clustered over a file cabinet brings an Asian feel to this corner, and an armoire adds height and scale while providing more storage.

BELOW Covered chests and wicker baskets in graduated sizes keep clutter out of sight and play up the Asian theme.

teahouse terrific

BRING ON THE LIGHT WITH A LITTLE IMAGINATION and not a lot of money, you can turn neglected parts of the house into inspiring "work areas" with pizzazz.

We had a small room that had four walls and no windows. That's right, no windows. So our task was to simulate real light and make the space feel bigger. Working from Layer One, Paint and Architecture, we first came up with a treatment for one entire wall using inexpensive wardrobe mirrors attached to the wall. This "shoji screen" treatment gave the room a decidedly Japanese look and visually doubled the space. We continued along that particular inspirational path.

In small spaces we think we can't use deep rich fabulous color because it will make the space too dark. But in this case all the light was artificial anyway, so we chose three compatible hues and went for it. Here, deep rich color provides

intimacy and literally redefines the space. These colors teamed with wonderful lighting (and don't forget those uplights) lead to a final effect that is warm and relaxing.

This room had an unusual airduct running diagonally along one wall from floor to ceiling. Here's where the art of disguise and illusion can really save the day. After doing our homework and reading about Japanese style, we created a "tokobashira" (alcove post) by covering the air duct with fake rough-hewn exterior siding, painted to look very antique. Then we took the elements of Japanese design and created a staggered shelf arrangement around the beam. Now we have fabulous storage and a very deliberate architectural element to play up our established Asian theme. When in doubt, be deliberate.

ABOVE For our original "shoji screen" wall, we added black-painted pine lathing strips to cover the mirror seams in a mullion pattern. Three panels run vertically and a horizontal panel unites them all the way across the wall, creating the effect of a transom. A little mirror magic can essentially double the entire space, as well as the light and the view.

For the work area, we constructed a long desk with two storage cubbies on each side. We positioned these shelves perpendicular to the wall from the top of the work surface to the ceiling. This also represents the "tokonoma," the place in Japanese homes to display an artistic ornament, usually an alcove at the end of a room. Now this fabulous storage space holds all of the office necessities and displays some decorative icons as well. And on the faces of the transom we installed three indoor fluorescent light fixtures enclosed in Plexiglas-fronted boxes. Normally these are designs for ceiling installation. We then painted the back of the Plexiglas with silhouettes of bamboo. How cool . . . and cheap.

With real estate as expensive as it is, every inch counts. Even a 10-by-10-foot space can become a productive environment rather than just a place to store unwanted clutter. But even more than that, it can also be a thought-provoking space that can nourish your soul.

During

ABOVE On the front of each shelf unit we mounted inexpensive workshop lights against the vertical surface. They are hinged to allow for easy access to change the fluorescent bulbs. To soften the light and further play up the theme, we reverse-painted a wonderful bamboo motif onto the opaque Plexiglas.

We resurfaced the top of the desk in a red-finish Formica. Comfortable seating at the desk and in an oversize upholstered leather side chair—yes, you can use large pieces of furniture in a small space—complete the functionality of the room.

OFFICE HOME AWAY FROM HOME ABOUT TO MOVE INTO our new offices, my team had a design huddle. With so much creative energy in our group, it seemed inappropriate for us to work in sterile surroundings. Even a stimulating workplace like the Christopher Lowell Show has stress. When we think of sanctuary spaces, we think of luxurious master bedrooms and baths, all very calming. Why not, we thought, take that sanctuary look and bring it into the office where we really need it?

Our goal in each 10-by-10-foot office space was to accommodate at least one person without office mates feeling as if they were on top of one another. Our goal was to promote bonding and productivity, while guarding individual privacy. We began with built-ins made from MDF (Medium Density Fiberboard) on opposite walls of the space. Then we designed a divider that provides storage and has a Plexiglas center to keep the space open, yet creates a sound barrier for privacy.

You always hear me say if you can't build out, build up. That's exactly what we did. We built counters at desk height around the perimeter of the room, narrowing them slightly under the windows. By building wall to wall you create a sort of cockpit effect and really maximize space. Above the desks on opposite walls, we built cubbyholes all the way up to hold the office supplies. Remember, part of reducing stress in the workplace is reducing clutter.

In one of the cockpit areas we painted the cubbyholes the same plum (Lowell Lavender) we used elsewhere against a green (Brined Grape Leaf) wall. We repeated the plum in the tonsu area, then reversed the colors on the other side. We love that!

Once we had our structure in place, it was all about surfaces. The desktops were covered in burlwood Formica for durability. The decorative design of the pattern introduces a connection to nature that reinforces the tranquil feeling. The front edges of the center wall divider were covered in faux bamboo and caning, in keeping with our use of organic elements elsewhere in the office (see directions for building this tonsu on page 120). Underneath the desks we made sure there was ample room for a couple of purchased file cabinets in fashion colors.

A group of bamboo-framed pictures above the desk picked up the bamboo on the tonsu. A few vases here and there, and fresh plants above, transform the corporate atmosphere with a cozy one. That's what makes us feel peaceful and relaxed even when our work is hectic.

Just about any space can be transformed into your very own mini-spiritual space. You don't have to sacrifice that tranquil feeling for form and function in the office when you surround yourself with comfortable, homey touches.

zensational office

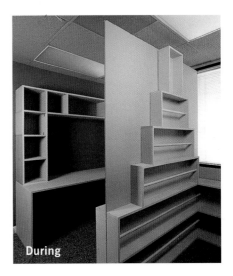

During

OPPOSITE In the center of the room is the divider between the two workstations. The divider is made up of two thin tonsu-like cases placed back to back with Plexiglas in the center—sort of like a big tonsu sandwich. Cool. Each person can see the co-worker on the other side, but can still carry on a private phone conversation. We added dowels to each shelf of the tonsus to create magazine racks. Now when we need reference material, it's always at our fingertips. You'll find step-by-step directions on page 120.

ABOVE AND RIGHT Here's a slight variation on the theme—who wants a cookie-cutter space? In this office we sandwiched Plexiglas between two low bookcases.

plexiglas tonsu
A DIVIDER WITH A DIFFERENCE

Eight 4-by-8-foot sheets ¾-inch MDF
   (Medium Density Fiberboard) or ply-
   wood
Sheet of Plexiglas
Wood glue
Wood screws
1-inch wood dowels (optional)
Table saw
Power drill/screwdriver
1-inch hole maker

NOTE: Build 2 of each individual
component of the tonsu.

The design of this shelving unit is very flexible. You can stack bookshelves, magazine racks, and plain wall dividers. The double-sided shelves maximize the use of space, and the Plexiglas (you could also use glass) provides privacy without blocking light

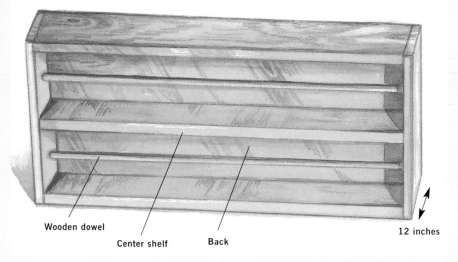

Wooden dowel

Center shelf   Back

12 inches

1. Start by constructing a bookcase from ¾-inch MDF or ¾-inch plywood approximately counter height by the desired length by a depth of 12 inches. Add a center shelf and a back to the bookcase. Secure all pieces with wood glue and screws.

2. If desired, drill a 1-inch diameter hole in the center halfway through the ends of each tier and place wooden dowels between the holes to hang magazines. The tiers could also be made deeper to accommodate square wicker baskets for storage.

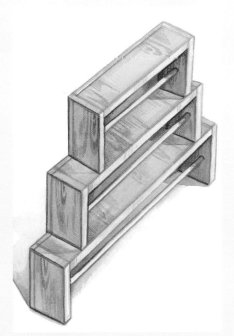

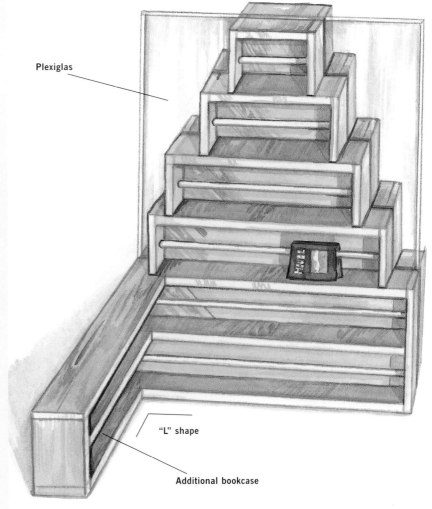

Plexiglas

"L" shape

Additional bookcase

3. Using ¾-inch MDF, build the next tier of the tonsu as a three-sided box with a back 1 foot shorter on each end than the bookcase foundation. Both the height and depth of each tier should be approximately 12 inches. Glue and screw all pieces together. Continue to build each tier 6 inches narrower on each end than the previous tier. Stack the tiers as a standard double stair-step configuration with each tier centered on the one below it. Or stack the tiers flush with one end and staggered at the opposite end. Attach the tiers together with wood glue and screws.

4. Build 2 complete tonsu units. Position them back to back and slide a piece of Plexiglas between them. Secure both units together through the Plexiglas with screws. If desired, construct 2 more bookcase units leaving one end open and secure them to the sides of the bookcase foundation in an "L" shape.

outdoor rooms

nature

Do you feel like a real

dummy when it comes

to the outdoors? Are

you two with nature?

Well believe it or not, you

don't have to be a

professional horticulturist

to create an outdoor space that's lush,

welcoming, and multifunctional. You just

dynamic

sanctuary

romantic

need to use the same tried-and-true techniques to

approach the patio, deck, or courtyard, as you

would your living room or bedroom. Build up layer

by layer, use the art of disguise to obscure ugly

features, create focal points,

and accessorize to your

own tastes. Still not

convinced you can do

it? Trust me on this

one, okay?

GREENERY

lush

party alfresco

Before

DRESSING UP THE OUT-OF-DOORS SO MANY OF YOU tell me that you share the same problem when it comes to entertaining alfresco. Your patio has accumulated a mishmash of outdoor furniture and you can't even make the space look organized, never mind elegant. This terrace is a good example of this dilemma. We looked at it and said, "Here's where old tables and chairs go to die." Our challenge was to find ways not only to make these unrelated furnishings look good as stand-alone pieces, but also to make them work together. The end result is what you see here.

First we needed to organize the space by dividing it into separate areas (that's right, Layer One is Paint and Architecture). Two prefabricated lattice panels placed in the right spot took care of that job. They not only shielded a potting and storage area from view, but also created a real entrance to the patio at large.

Overgrown vines covered an ugly chain-link fence on one side of the patio. (Let's face it. There's no such thing as a beautiful chain-link fence.) To make this one go away, we cut back all the old brush and sprayed the stumps with Round Up, a relatively nontoxic herbicide, to keep the brush from growing back. Then we took more lattice panels and wired them to the fence with heavy-gauge wire. A new bougainvillea on top, and—presto—a touch of the tropical. (If you live a little too far north for bougainvillea, try an ivy or a trumpet vine instead.)

OPPOSITE When designing an outdoor retreat, remember that the eye goes to color, so use splashes of it to draw attention from one conversation area to another, spreading the color evenly around the entire space.

RIGHT A truly happening party spot calls for plenty of places to set down food and drinks. Because you also need a place to relax and enjoy nature, we created a restful niche by surrounding a sunflower Adirondack chair with complementary containers overflowing with flowers.

Getting back to the center of the action, we created a series of conversation areas by grouping together furniture and plant-filled containers. You can see that we haven't just placed our containers randomly, we've clustered them together. Remember, there's drama in mass.

Another important space is the outdoor "kitchen." Here, our trusty Weber Genesis barbecue became the nucleus of activity. Why? Because just as in an indoor kitchen, people gather around. Now the chef can feel like part of the festivities. We considered renovating the existing table, but after doing the math we realized that buying a new unfinished table and covering the top with tile mosaics was actually cheaper.

ABOVE You don't need plants in every container. These tall urns look just fine flanking either side of the workspace entrance. But you could fill them with dramatic arrangements for special occasions.

ABOVE RIGHT AND RIGHT A good outdoor dinner party requires good lighting, and you can't beat candles and votives for evening light. Not only are they flattering and romantic, but you don't have to plug them in. Twinkling white lights, used mostly at Christmas, can add "firefly" sparkle to any outdoor environment.

One thing that really makes this area stand out is the hand-painted umbrella. It's a single item that adds height, scale, and color to the space. This look can be easily replicated with a market umbrella sold at import and many garden stores and decorated with fabric paint. You can do it!

goof-proof containers

I love container gardening, but until I learned a few simple rules, I couldn't keep the plants inside them happy. But if all else fails, remember that faltering foliage can always be replaced with new plants. Bye-bye now!

- Plants in containers need lots of room, so buy the biggest pots you can afford.

- Plastic and Styrofoam pots are lighter and often cheaper than terra-cotta or ceramic, plus they don't freeze and crack in winter. But look for the nicest "faux" pots you can find. There are choices on the market now that are virtually indistinguishable from their heavier counterparts.

- Make sure there are drainage holes in the bottom of the pot. Otherwise you'll drown your plants.

- Place an empty nursery container upside down in the bottom of your pot before filling it with soil. The extra volume creates air space and helps keep the larger container light.

- Don't skimp on potting mix: Buy a quality, premixed potting soil that contains peat moss to retain water and perlite to lighten the mix and improve air circulation.

- Add a handful of slow-release fertilizer when planting. It will feed your plants for you.

- Design your foliage layout using basic shapes: mounding, tall, and draping. Put the tall plant in the middle, surround it with mounding plants, and let the draping plants trail over the container's edges.

- Finally, unless you have the time to water your containers regularly, invest in an inexpensive irrigation system with an automatic timer. Conceal the plastic tubing behind the pots and make sure each pot gets its own emitter. Drinks on tap!

the art of disguise

OUTDOOR ILLUSIONS JUST AS WE SOMETIMES FIND funny little rooms indoors, we also see some pretty challenging outdoor spaces. This patio was a good example of an awkward, even ugly spot. It was small and enclosed with an old, faded fence. The dimensions of the lot are uneven, with many different angles. Consequently there was a lot of wasted space. But perhaps the worst aspect was the concrete slab, which had buckled and cracked with time. You might look at a place like this and think it's a hopeless case. But never say never! The owner of this patio dreamed of a romantic outdoor retreat, cozy and candlelit. Well, I could see that we had at least two of the right criteria—the space was snug and had a feeling of enclosure. We just needed to turn these elements to our advantage.

The big task here was to deal with the surfaces. This cracked slab may look like a job for a couple of brawny guys and a sledgehammer, but removing concrete is really expensive. In fact, it costs more to remove concrete than to pour it. That didn't exactly work with the owner's budget, so we needed to think of some clever ways to use the art of disguise. And that ugly fence was serving a purpose—it blocked the neighbors' view as well as obtrusive traffic noises—but it needed to be transformed from functional to fun.

Because of the effects of wear and tear, not to mention weather, the paint on outdoor surfaces has to be a lot tougher than paint on walls and floors indoors. There's no point

Before

in trying to achieve a uniform surface, so we worked around the defects. First, we created a background that suggested dappled shade by using two different values of green. Then we really turned our imaginations loose and created some special effects on the stairs and underneath the patio table.

OPPOSITE Tall tables add height rather than weight; perfect for small spaces like this.

Cement paints used to be available only in a few garish colors. That range is now expanding, but remember, there is nothing wrong with bright color

ABOVE LEFT AND RIGHT Think of all the things you can paint on outdoor surfaces. Hang "artwork" just as you would indoors and let vines clamber around them. This shows what you can do with an existing feature. Ask yourself, "Is it really nice enough as is?"

outdoors. On the stairs, we used several different primary colors to make a faux-mosaic pattern. The result draws you down the steps into the patio. Then we used similar paint colors to make the "area rug" underneath the table. Once again, the eye is drawn to that focal point.

Next we tackled that tired old fence. First we covered it with a good coat of primer followed by a buttery yellow that would look warm and romantic by candlelight. Painting a detailed, artistic effect directly on the walls can be tricky, so instead we decided to try something a little different. The frescoes are actually stencils painted onto luan—a material with a thin applied veneer—then screwed directly onto the wall. One scene is a pastoral landscape and the other is a very real-looking fountain. You can use this technique to make indoor relief frescoes as well. It's a perfect element for an entryway or a transitional space to the outdoors. Just make sure you seal the work with polyurethane.

To integrate the fountain fresco with its surroundings, we took an existing planter, painted it, and applied some relief stencils to the front. These stencils really give a three-dimensional look. We took an old birdbath, filled it with floating candles, and—voilà! Instant antiquity. We also "framed" our frescoes with tall potted plants. These add height, scale, and symmetry to the perimeter.

Even I know you can't plant anything in concrete, so our garden grows in containers. We placed them in groups and used tall standards—flowering plants that have been pruned up—to create dots of color. The table and chairs are bar height—perfect for a little tête-a-tête in the garden. And for that touch of atmosphere and romance, we placed candles everywhere—floating candles, luminarias, and even a chandelier hanging overhead from a tree branch.

From eyesore to oasis, this yard comes into its own at night. It's warm, it's cozy, it's romantic, and it's right outside the back door!

ABOVE LEFT Instead of feeling like the stairway to the dungeon, these painted steps are now an inviting pathway to an enchanted space. **TOP RIGHT** We repeated the faux mosaic pattern on the *chiminea,* a Mexican outdoor fireplace. That's another way to spruce up an otherwise uninspired object. **ABOVE RIGHT** Why not have an outdoor rug? It will never fade or need to be cleaned. Just be sure you use durable concrete paint.

mediterranean magic

Before

OPPOSITE This is the front walkway that leads to the door. The tile is now tied into the rest of the garden.

WHEN FORMAL MEETS FUNCTIONAL | GET LETTERS from so many of you telling me that you just don't know where to begin when it comes to the outdoors. Well, just as you sometimes need to get other people involved when doing your room interiors, it can really be a big help if you get others involved with your exteriors, too. This "outdoor room" on a small suburban lot is a good example of this process.

What the owner of this house wanted more than anything else was low maintenance, and that's true for a lot of us. Needy spaces? Puh-lease! The original lot was basically a square piece of lawn that needed to be mowed, watered, and fed regularly, tasks the owner simply didn't have time to do. He also wanted something that would be a little more in keeping with the architecture of his house, which is a contemporary Mediterranean style. This is *always* something to consider when designing an outdoor space. If you have a house with a very distinctive architectural style, it's best to match the landscaping to that look. A cottage garden can look out of place beside an ultramodern home, for example. It's like outfitting a sleek monochrome room with fussy taffeta curtains. Don't go there!

Not knowing where to begin, the owner turned for help to a landscape design firm. The first thing the firm did was to come up with a plan on paper showing the basic "hardscape," that is, the overall outlines and structural elements they were proposing for the garden, along with a list of plants. It's a good idea to ask for the plan in color so you can really see what you're getting. The colors in this design were soft, muted terra-cottas and tans, perfectly matched to the house. In place of a lawn, the landscape designer indicated a paved area of decomposed granite surrounded by a row of saltillo tiles and a border of gray-leafed plants. This garden went from being a needy water-guzzler to using very little water and requiring virtually no upkeep. That's my kind of garden—it takes care of itself.

It's not as important to know the Latin names of the plants as it is to choose those that are well matched to the site. In our dry and hot climate of California, drought-resistant plants were put into service, of course. Nature designed these species to drink very little water, and their colors matched the palette of the house and garden. Because the plan was bold, with simple lines, it also called for plants with a strong structural appearance. In other words, no pansies or petunias! Aloes and other succulents are well suited to this purpose, as are lavender, grasses, New Zealand flax, and similar plants that originate in hot climates. The designer also chose plants that would harmonize with the formal, symmetrical look of the garden, and kept it to a few choice varieties to give an overall cohesive look. Depending on what part of the country you live in, you should always

adapt your planting scheme to the perennials and shrubs that will thrive in your climate. Visit your local nursery for suggestions.

When you have a garden designed for you by a professional, you can choose to do the installation yourself or have a landscaping firm do it for you. For instance the decomposed granite that forms the interior surface of this courtyard is inexpensive and fairly easy to work with, but unless you feel comfortable with masonry, it's best to let a professional lay tiles, dig ponds, and install drainage systems. Any time you enlist the help of a design professional for your interior or exterior rooms, look for guidance from somebody who wants to be a partner with you in the project rather than dictate to you how it should be done. After all, you're the one who has to live with the results long after a professional has gone. It's best to have a written contract, signed by both parties, spelling out exactly what services are to be provided. Typically, for a landscape design job such as this, the design will be included with the installation. Give the designer one-third of the agreed fee as a deposit, another third after the hardscape is complete, and the

ABOVE LEFT AND RIGHT These very cool and modern aluminum benches look great in this formal garden. Imagine how different it would look if these were the usual teak?

remainder when the plants are all in the ground. Most landscape professionals will guarantee their plants, as long as you follow care guidelines.

Once you have the basic architecture of your garden established and the plant palette chosen, it's time to accessorize the space. In tune with the formality of this garden, the designer placed matching benches at either end. To alter the fountain so that the water flows out over the top, we dug a trench and installed a liner (these are available at garden- and pond-supply stores), then fitted over it a grate that would support the fountain. The pump had to be sufficiently large to recirculate water up from the lined trench through the fountain.

Finally, just as you would implement Layer Seven indoors, the last step in your garden design is lighting. In this courtyard, uplights really add a touch of elegance at dusk. The overall effect is very simple, but very charming and perfectly suited to the site. What was an uninteresting high-maintenance garden, barely noticeable through the window, has now become an elegant surprise to all those who venture past the front gates.

ABOVE LEFT AND RIGHT No garden is complete without a fountain. The sound of running water is one of the most soothing things in the world. To create your own indoor or outdoor water fountain, see the step-by-step instructions on page 136. (Note: These photos were taken eight months after the initial planting.)

saucer fountain

WATER TRICKLES THROUGH IT

Large terra-cotta saucer (about 24
  inches in diameter and at least 4
  inches deep)

Small fountain pump

Snap-on electric plug replacement

Clear plastic tubing

River rocks or polished stones

12-inch piece of 4-inch-diameter
  bamboo

8-inch piece of 1-inch-diameter bamboo

Short 3/8-inch-diameter bamboo stick for
  cotter pin

Potted water plants and grasses

Bamboo plant supports

Power drill with 3/8-inch masonry bit
  and 1-inch hole saw

Power saw

Scissors

Clear-coat protective sealer

Paintbrush

Wire cutters

Utility knife

When it comes to winding down at the end of the day, there's nothing more soothing than the gentle splashing of water in a fountain. Fountains are for sale everywhere these days, it seems, but they can be expensive. You really don't have to know much about waterworks to make one that actually works. Whether you use it indoors or out, it will be a fabulous addition to your home.

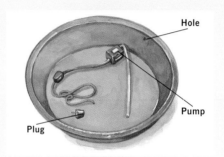

Hole

Pump

Plug

1. If the saucer is unglazed, seal the inside and outside with several coats of protective sealer. Let dry between each coat. Drill a hole in the side close to the rim using a masonry drill bit. Snip the plug off the pump with wire cutters. Feed the end of the cord through the hole in the saucer from the inside out. Replace the plug with a snap-on plug following the package directions.

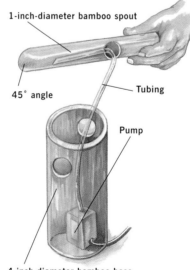

1-inch-diameter bamboo spout

45° angle

Tubing

Pump

4-inch-diameter bamboo base

2. For the base, drill a 1-inch hole in the 4-inch-diameter bamboo piece approximately 3 inches from the top. Drill another 1-inch hole on the opposite side slightly higher than the first. Then cut the end of the 1-inch-diameter piece of bamboo at a 45-degree angle (for a water spout) and drill a 1-inch hole midway on the longer side. Drill two 3/8-inch holes on opposite sides of the 1-inch bamboo 1 inch from the straight cut edge. The base will fit over the pump and the tubing will be threaded up through the base and the spout.

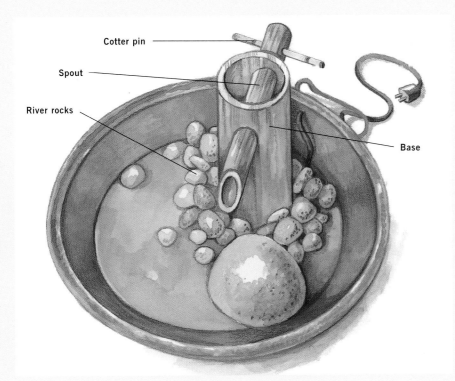

Cotter pin

Spout

River rocks

Base

3. Feed the spout through the holes in the base from the outer edge of the saucer so the spout points toward the center. Manipulate the tubing as needed so that it extends almost to the end of the spout. Secure the bamboo pieces by pushing the bamboo cotter pin through the small holes in the 1-inch-diameter bamboo piece. Place river rocks or stones in the saucer.

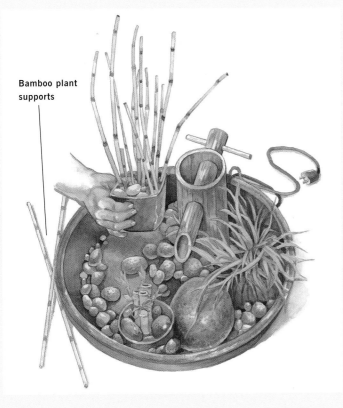

Bamboo plant supports

4. Place plastic pots of water plants and grasses into the saucer in a pleasing arrangement. Put gravel over the soil. If the rims of the pots protrude above the waterline, cut them down to soil level using a utility knife. Fill the saucer with water to a level just below the cord hole. As a finishing touch, lay bamboo plant supports across the top of the saucer.

from the outside in

You dream of tending

blooming orchids

and clambering vines, of

sipping tea in graceful surroundings, of

filling the house with fresh bouquets.

But the last thing you want to do is

get your boots dirty! Now there's a solution for

people who love plants but like to keep their feet

dry—the conservatory. Advances in technology and

jungle

construction have put paid to the common complaints of traditional glass houses—too hot in summer, too cold in winter. We'll show you how to create a garden room that's at once a horticultural delight and a practical room addition. And we'll show you how to integrate it with the rest of the house.

stone

in transit

MAKING A SMOOTH TRANSITION WHAT DO YOU DO with transitional spaces? You know, those entry halls or passageways that really don't function as rooms, but more as spaces between rooms? The best place to look for inspiration for these areas might be out in the "real" world. Each year we devote an entire show to great ideas from public spaces, taking our cues from professional architects—after all, who knows better then commercial designers how to handle such a "just-passing-through" configuration? So I decided to take a trip. After venturing out and making a tour of a few hotel lobbies, a theater, and an office reception area, I came back with tons of options. Remember, with public spaces you don't have to check in to check it out.

This room serves as a transition from the conservatory shown on the following pages to the rest of our studio house, functioning partly as a hallway and partly as an entryway. To translate the indoor-outdoor garden feeling into the hall, we decided to turn it into an indoor courtyard.

Immediately we thought of stone. How great it would be to have big slabs of sandstone lining the walls and floor! But the expense would be prohibitive, not to mention that the weight of the stone would probably pull the walls down. So we consulted with our master scenic painter, Steven Burright. He quickly suggested a floor-to-ceiling trompe l'oeil effect that would mimic the look of weighty cut stone. I told him I didn't want the room to look like some medieval dungeon, so we came up with the mental imagery of a spa in a great hotel. The colors would be light and creamy, and the lines would be straight and precise, rather than rustic and antique.

Steven began by face-coating the walls with a deep gray paint to simulate grout lines. With a plumb line, he marked out a stone pattern, then simulated the outline of individual bricks with narrow masking tape. Then he troweled on two thin coats of Flex-all (a premixed wet patching compound available in most hardware stores) tinted with universal pigment. You can apply the material more thickly for a greater three-dimensional effect. After the Flex-all had set slightly, but not dried, Steven removed the tape. With a dry brush, he then gave the entire surface a brown, white, and pale yellow spatter to create a slightly distressed and pitted effect. Finally, he used gray paint slightly darker than the "grout" lines to accentuate the shadows. Sensational!

Now it was time to add the real (and much more affordable) architectural elements. Several turns of crown molding were installed to create an overhead ledge that added a high-end spa feeling. It also helped soften the "stonework."

During

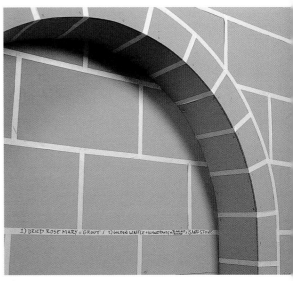

1) DRIED ROSE MARY = GROUT / 2) GOLDEN WAFFLE + ALMOND PASTE (WORLD?) SANDSTONE

We next added a fiber-optic rope light and plants to the upper ledges on the crown molding shelves. These filigree wall sconces are a chic cheat—facsimiles of those big, heavy wrought-iron pieces that you see in outdoor courtyards. Ours cost $40 instead of $600. We made the facsimiles by drawing and painting the design on pieces of thin luan, then screwing these pieces to the walls. We then mounted our inexpensive electrical fixtures onto the faux iron back plates. This adds more relief than if you paint directly on the wall surface. We used a similar technique in other outdoor areas (see page 130).

We brought some of the same touches we used in the conservatory into this inner courtyard, too. The wrought-iron benches lining the walls, for instance, are pushed up against the edges of the room to allow easy passage. Likewise, the candle chandelier hanging from the ceiling resembles one found in the next room. And then there are the tall topiary and sculptural plants placed around the perimeter and flanking the doorway into the glass house. Think of waiting in a lobby for a date or an appointment—you need somewhere to sit and look nonchalant, right? Based on this idea, we built this wonderful circular pouf for the center of our transitional space. (*Pouf* is French for a great big ottoman with a center support.) Upholstered in a chocolate-colored fabric with copper silk throw pillows, this addition lent function to the room. It's a perfect public-private piece that allows you to sit comfortably yet somewhat formally. Ooh la la.

ABOVE LEFT With the pouf and the benches, this is an ideal space for cocktails before dinner, where guests can form different conversation groups rather than all facing one another in a circle. It's become one of our favorite spaces. You can bet we'll be having our Christmas party here. Cheers!
ABOVE RIGHT The wall with the background color in place, taped off ready for the faux finish.

circular pouf
MAKE AN ENTRANCE GRAND

This upholstered centerpiece is known as a pouf and it has many uses. It can serve as a seat, a low table, or simply as the centerpiece of an entryway. We made our version a generous 5 feet across but you can adjust the dimensions to suit your space. If you reduce the diameter to less than 4 feet, eliminate the backrest in favor of a greater seating area.

Three 4-by-8-foot sheets ¾-inch MDF
   (Medium Density Fiberboard) or
   plywood
2 sheets ¼-inch wiggle board
One 4-by-8-foot sheet ¼-inch luan
1-by-3-inch wood strips
6 wood legs with screw-in ends
1½-inch upholstery foam
Upholstery fabric (solid color)
Quilt batting
Kraft paper, pencil, and scissors
Wood glue
Wood screws
Spray adhesive
Staple gun and staples
Jigsaw
Power drill with screwdriver bit

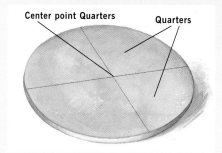

Center point Quarters   Quarters

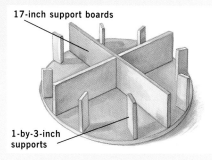

17-inch support boards

1-by-3-inch supports

1. For the seat, cut 2 circles from MDF or plywood to the desired dimensions. Mark both circles into quarters by first finding the center point and then drawing 2 lines at 90-degree angles through this point.

2. Cut MDF or plywood support boards to fit along the quadrant markings on the base (we made ours 17 inches high). Attach them using wood glue and then screwing from below. Then attach 2 additional 1-by-3-inch supports for each quadrant.

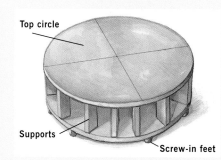

Top circle

Supports

Screw-in feet

3. Lay glue along the top of all the supports, set the top circle in place, then secure it with wood screws. Around the base circle, attach the 6 screw-in feet, equally spaced.

Wiggle board

4. Complete the seat by cutting a strip of wiggle board equal in length to the circumference of the seat. Secure it around the base, gluing and then screwing to the wood supports.

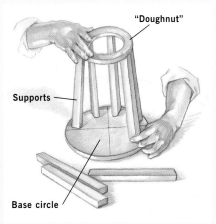

"Doughnut"

Supports

Base circle

5. Construct the cone-shaped center backrest by first cutting a circle from MDF or plywood to the desired dimensions (slightly less than $\frac{1}{3}$ the diameter of the seat circle) for the base. Then cut a top "doughnut" slightly smaller in diameter than the base. Cut nine 1-by-3-inch upright supports, angling the ends slightly to achieve a taper. Glue and screw the supports around the base of the cone. Screw the "doughnut" to the top of the supports.

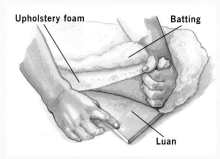

Wiggle board

6. Make a paper pattern of the backrest by placing the cone on its side on a sheet of kraft paper. Mark a beginning point and roll the cone along the paper, marking both the top and bottom edges. Cut wiggle board to the template shape, then wrap it around the backrest. Use the same template to cut upholstery foam, then adhere the foam to the backrest with spray adhesive. Cover with quilt batting. Cut upholstery fabric to the shape of the pattern, adding a 2-inch seam allowance to all sides. With right sides together, stitch the cone-shaped fabric along the side edge. Turn right side out and stretch the upholstery fabric around the backrest. Turn the raw edges under and staple to the inside top and bottom of the backrest.

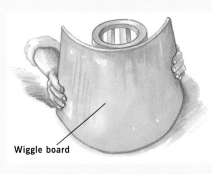

Upholstery foam

Batting

Luan

7. Before making the seat cushions, center the backrest on the seat and reach down through the "doughnut" to secure the backrest to the seat with wood screws. Cap the backrest with a fabric-covered disc. Then cut a kraft paper seat pattern in the shape of one quadrant of the seat, curving the inner edge around the center backrest. Use the pattern to cut 4 cushions of luan and upholstery foam (or have the foam cut for you by the supplier); glue the foam to the luan. Cover the foam with batting.

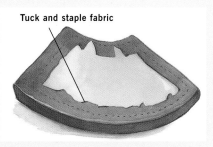

Tuck and staple fabric

8. Cover each cushion with upholstery fabric, tucking and stapling it to the underside of the cushion. Upholster the sides of the pouf by covering the wiggle board with batting and then fabric. Tuck the fabric under and on top of the seat and staple in place. Finally, take the four cushions and position them around the pouf. Voilà!

solar sanctuary

A GARDEN ROOM COMES INTO ITS OWN ONE OF the most popular and useful ideas for expanding living space is to add a solarium or sunroom. You know—rooms made mostly of glass for that indoor-outdoor feel? Real estate agents tell us that a sunroom vastly improves the curb appeal of a home. Well, when we decided to get rid of the kitchen in our studio house, it gave us a wonderful space with which to work. The question was, what would we build instead?

My previous experience with sunrooms, or conservatories as they are traditionally called, was not good. They were leaky, drafty, and either too hot in summer or too cold in winter. But new materials and construction styles have turned these structures into the hottest (or coolest) thing in home additions. When we got an offer from our friends at Four Seasons Sunrooms, we decided to go ahead. We took a custom-built conservatory and created a romantic, exotic space— one that is at once part of the house and yet separate from it. The area where the kitchen had been became a transitional space, and we broke through the kitchen's window and wall to open up a 10-foot doorway. Now it was time to choose a style.

Conservatories range from Victorian to ultramodern. Because our house is a traditional Colonial style, we opted for a rectangular space that ends in an octagon. Its high-pitched glass ceiling with fanlike beams reminded us of turn-of-the-century conservatories found in a grand manor. We also opted for 2-foot "knee" walls and connecting French doors that lead out onto the garden.

Before

The great thing about wood (as opposed to vinyl or aluminum framing) is that it can be more easily painted or stained, so that you can really individualize the space. We painted ours the same yellow and cream as the inner courtyard.

You don't want to feel like a bug under a magnifying glass in an all-glazed room, so some kind of shading is essential. We added matchstick import blinds all around. To cover the floor, we extended our existing wood veneer floors out over the newly poured concrete foundation. We chose a carpet with a pattern of two-tone café au lait, warm yet subtly suggestive of a dappled-shade leaf pattern.

Naturally we wanted to fill the environment with plants, but we also wanted to keep everything in containers in case we needed to move them. All of the containers came with saucers to protect the floor. Since plants are the major feature of this room, we chose a variety of leaf shapes and textures to help create the feel-

During

ing of a real jungle. To reduce maintenance, we bought several tall trees from an artificial foliage supplier (who knew?) and mixed them with medium-sized shrubs and houseplants. This combination gave us the height and drama needed to furnish the space without having to worry about the trees someday outgrowing the space. Help keep your real container plants healthy by following the simple guidelines on page 127.

For me, it's the wrought-iron details that really make this space. A fabulous set of patterned doors hang at the entrance, complemented by a bar-height weathered iron table and chairs and matching folding screen. The hands-down centerpiece of this romantic retreat is a wonderful distressed metal daybed, designed and donated by our friend Kathy Ireland. Most important, we now have a place to commune with nature without ever having to go outside.

LEFT The daybed makes the room. It adds an upholstered element and has become the perfect place for us to sit and relax, or even to film the opening of my show.

BELOW FAR LEFT With greenery cascading everywhere, colorful fruit and flower displays are especially appropriate.

BELOW LEFT Don't spend a lot on an indoor garden room and then skimp on the containers. Look for quality reproduction urns and pots rather than cheap plastic ones.

OPPOSITE ABOVE The wrought-iron gates look ancient, but in fact they are reproductions that we had made for approximately one-third the cost of the originals. What a spectacular way to make an entrance.

OPPOSITE BELOW Old-fashioned touches like this flower-filled miniature glass house remind us of the timelessness of nature.

someone's in the kitchen

serious
chef

When it comes to kitchen

redesign, it's easy to break

the budget in a hurry. So

much of the expense involved in the

remodel is in the upgrade of surfaces.

Cabinets, countertops, floors, to

STAINLESS STEEL

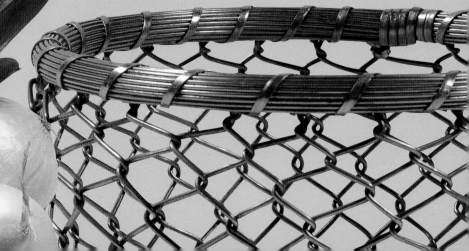

warmth

cuisine

say nothing of the appliances, can be

those big-budget items that postpone

your dreams of a redo. Once

again, that's where the

art of disguise—and a

little cleverness—

can work wonders.

gourmet upgrade

THIS KITCHEN MAKEOVER began as a dark, dingy apartment space that was in desperate need of updating.

The wood cabinets had to stay—this apartment was a rental. So we painted them a beautiful warm buttery color. The fresh paint colors, including sage green for the wall and a fun green combination on the ceiling, made a huge difference in the room's "attitude." Paint is still the cheapest, most effective way to retheme any room. And remember, just because it's wood doesn't mean it's good. The minute you decide to paint, you open up infinite possibilities.

Fortunately, this kitchen had some good points. We were blessed with white tile countertops that were in fine shape. We decided not only to keep these, but also to incorporate white accents throughout the room.

The money saved by not ripping out the counters was used to upgrade the dishwasher with a stainless-steel front and replace the range with a serious, high-grade restaurant stove with a matching stainless-steel hood. We replaced the panels on the refrigerator with matching stainless-steel ones, to coordinate the look.

Then we covered the existing old linoleum with interlocking veneer wood flooring. This was key. The minute we put down the floor, the space instantly took on a charming old farmhouse feeling. We moderated a not-so-great view out the kitchen window by building a little shelf combination made out of aluminum tubing and Plexiglas. The step-down design allows light to come in and shine through the owner's collection of colored bottles and glasses, making patterns all over the kitchen. And we can still see into the courtyard outside.

We organized counter clutter by placing everything on trays. They're easy to move for cleaning and make instant order out of what was previously a disorganized mess. Above all, kitchens are working areas. When your workspace is well organized and uncluttered, your work will go smoothly.

Before

OPPOSITE Can you combine an old-world look with modern appliances? Well let's face it, most of us can't afford to buy antique or even reproduction appliances. Refrigerators, stoves, and dishwashers are kitchen elements that are unavoidably contemporary. Sometimes its better to play up a feature than to try to hide it. By pairing this kitchen's hand-hued plank flooring with new stainless-steel faces for the appliances, we created a wonderful contrast.

LEFT Part of bringing personality to a space is by merchandizing. Here, ordinary objects combine with one-of-a-kind pieces to create great "eye candy."

OPPOSITE These shelves add interest to a plain window, but block a minimal amount of light. They're simply aluminum tubes threaded through Plexiglas shelves. You can use wooden dowels or copper pipe instead of the aluminum, if that suits your kitchen décor. The same kind of shelves make great CD racks elsewhere in the house, too.

kitchen
à la
carte

WHEN WE INHERITED the kitchen in our Universal studio home, it didn't look like an inviting place to cook, much less like a room that should be the warm center of the house. First of all, the cabinets were laminated with a pickled effect that looked rather charmless. Because the cabinets were out of scale with the height of the ceilings, we wanted to extend them. Our goal was to add a sense of antique architecture and create display space for attractive serving pieces that take up valuable cupboard space. In addition, the different cabinets looked disconnected. We hoped that our "add to" adornments would save the day—and the wallet.

To begin with, we repainted the existing cabinets with a crackle finish. We began with a base coat of yellow, then added the crackle medium, and then applied a topcoat of soft blues and greens. Because we had to remove the cabinet doors in order to paint them, we decided to remove the inner panels of the doors and add even more inside display space to the cupboards. The first year, we stapled chicken wire to the inside of the doors for a French country feeling. Then the next year we replaced the chicken wire with frosted etched glass to add a high-tech element to the room. They don't look overly industrial, but they have a clean, modern appearance. You can see how we did this below.

To further add to the existing cabinets, we made a series of pine boxes. We faced the front of each box with sheets of faux bead board, cutting an arched shape that would later be refined with molding. These boxes would rest directly on top of the existing cabinets.

With our cabinets done and our new arches installed and trimmed, we then added a jabot and swag window treatment over the sink to soften the area and connect all the elements together. In the arches above, we attached the same fabric in a fanlike shape as a background for more merchandise opportunities.

We also inherited a plain old plywood floor that had previously been stained. That's right, a stained plywood floor. It was one of those elements that look bad no matter what you do to them. To give the kitchen a bit of drama and contrast, we used very inexpensive black and white peel-and-stick tile over the existing floor. We also added a lovely big island in the center of the room for additional work surface and storage. This also allowed us to install a great hanging pot rack, which further unburdened valuable cupboard space.

The countertops were very deep blue Formica. Now let me tell you something: If you get to pick the color of a kitchen counter surface, think in terms of neutral colors. Earmarking a large counter with deep color influences everything else you do in the room. Because we had spent so little money so far, we decided

to spend a little to tile both the backsplash and counter surfaces in shades of soft green and buttery gold.

As we moved into the second year of our Universal home, we updated the kitchen to a more high-tech look by adding a stainless-steel sink and stainless-steel accessories. We added brand-new slick modern pieces of hardware on the cabinets and light strip molding around the perimeter of the insides of the cabinets. It was a great way to light up the background and play up the colorful glassware inside. We replaced the panels on the refrigerator with aluminum ones we got from an install-it-yourself kit to add to the high-tech appearance. Great for those old avocado green appliances.

ABOVE Using the art of disguise, we "added to" existing elements rather than "ripping out," and we saved a ton of money that we could then use on elements of the kitchen that really needed replacing. This room went from charmless to romantic to high-tech for a fraction of the cost. Who knew?

cabinet upgrade
A NEW FACE IN THE KITCHEN

1-by-2-inch pine strips

½-inch aluminum angle stripping

Glass cut to inside dimensions of frame or cabinet door opening

Self-adhesive frosted film, Con-Tact paper, or glass etching products

Door-hanging hardware (hinges and handles)

Silicone and caulking gun

Wood glue

Miter saw or miter box and handsaw

Power drill and screwdriver

Screws or nails and hammer

Clean rag and rubbing alcohol

How many ways can you think of to dress up your kitchen cabinets? Not only could you paint or reface them, but you can also make them see-through. What adds that personal touch, however, is using a material that's transparent yet interesting. Chicken wire, fabric, glass— plain, frosted, or patterned; you can fill in the basic frame of your cabinets with anything that catches your fancy. The instructions here are for making a frame from scratch; you could also remove and replace the interior panel of some existing cupboards.

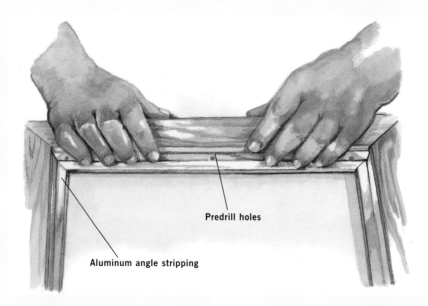

Predrill holes

Aluminum angle stripping

1. Determine the outside measurements of the cabinet doors and cut 4 pine strips for the sides, mitering each corner. Glue and screw or nail the boards together at the corners; finish the wood as desired. (We base-coated the doors, applied crackle medium, and added a contrasting topcoat of paint.) Cut the aluminum angle stripping to the inside dimensions of the cabinet door opening, mitering the corners. Predrill holes along the inside edges of the angle stripping and wood frame and screw or nail the angle stripping pieces to the frame.

Drop in glass insert

2. Glass inserts can be precut to match the dimensions of your frame. Apply peel-and-stick frosted film, Con-Tact paper, or glass etching products to on side of the glass.

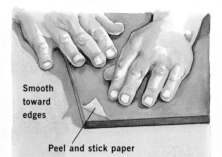

Smooth toward edges

Peel and stick paper

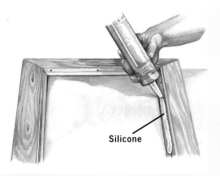

Silicone

3. Place a bead of silicone along the aluminum angle channel. Use a rag to wipe off excess silicone and to push the silicone deep into the corner of the channel (alcohol can remove any spills of silicone). Drop the glass insert into the silicone bead so that the covered or etched side of the glass faces inward, toward the inside of the cabinet.

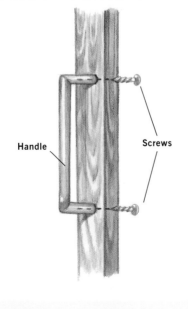

Handle   Screws

4. Screw the hinges onto the doors and attach to the cabinet fascia. Drill holes into the door frame and insert hardware as desired.

fun and games

It's true. I have on occasion been accused

of going over the top. Well, I say, why not?

I can't think of a more perfect place

to go over the top than in a kid's

room. It's really a situation where you can

get a little outrageous, have a good time,

and not take things too seriously. The

inspiration? Being fearless, not appropriate.

NURTURE

cool

laughter

bright

After all, kids deserve

to have their dreams come

true, too. But remember the golden

rules for kids' rooms: They must be

durable, accessible, and safe.

sweet dreams

A ROOM THAT WILL GROW WITH BABY SO YOU'RE GOING TO have a baby. What a set of completely new life challenges this will bring and, needless to say, I don't mean just the décor. Think of all the paraphernalia an infant needs—the changing table, the crib, the rocking chair, and on and on and on. How is it all going to fit into a teeny little 8-by-8-foot room? And what happens when your little one grows up and wants something a little less babyish?

Our job is to make sure this is a perfect space for an infant; that it is warm and cozy and tranquil and does all the things that a child needs done. More important, it shouldn't require a total redo once the child begins to grow. As a toddler he or she will want lots of the latest new gadgets designed to entertain and improve intelligence, along with all the soft, cuddly stuffed animals.

The first thing we did was paint the room a dusty blueberry color—not the usual standard "baby blue." Choosing an "adult color" means you won't have to repaint a year or two later when you update the décor. Kids' rooms contain lots of colorful artwork and objects that compete for attention, so the wall color will simply serve as background. The ceiling color is a soft taffy tan that we used as the wall color in the adjoining bathroom. They go together because they're the same value. (Remember how I'm always telling you to reverse the ceiling and wall colors in rooms next to each other?) We left the existing trim white to unite the space.

The ceiling in the room was very tall. We had plenty of overhead space to put up plain pine shelving supported by "L" brackets around three walls of the room above the window casing. Then we cut puffy cloud shapes out of luan, a thin wood veneer, painted them, and attached them to the fronts of the shelves. What a great storage concept—taller objects look great as they peek over the clouds, and not-so-decorative stuff is concealed behind.

The focal point of the whole window treatment is the sunburst painted directly on the wall over the window. A pole and cup system below the shelf supports panels of plaid fabric on either side of the window. Below the sunburst are panels of sheer fabric with a subtle floral pattern. This simple treatment allows the light to shine in but blocks the view of some not-so-kid-friendly corporate office building across the street. The window treatment is non-gender-specific and won't need to be replaced as the child matures. You gotta think ahead.

Furniture placement was key in this small space. We put the crib at an angle in the corner so baby could see the

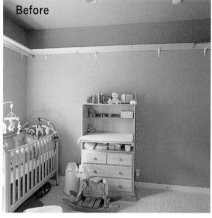

Before

light and dancing flowers in the window. The changing table and additional storage for baby clothes and other necessities were situated on the wall opposite the crib. And a comfy rocking chair filled out the corner. As the child gets older, the chair can move to the other side of the room and a twin bed can go in front of the window, with the window treatment becoming a cornice over the head.

With very little money, some planning for the future, and a lot of imagination we have been able to pull together a space that will grow as the child does. By creating such special places for your children, you'll encourage them to stay put in their own beds rather than running into your room at night. The parents of little Alexander tell me that since birth he's slept nowhere but here. I feel like a proud uncle!

ABOVE LEFT AND ABOVE The fabric panels really warm up this space, making it cozy and comforting for a little one. And because babies spend a lot of time lying down, there's plenty to look up at.

BACK TO THE FUTURE THIS ROOM IS SO COOL. It's a little spaceship, a little 1950s retro, and a lot of fun. We think it's a terrific example of how you can spruce up a kid's room to create an imaginative environment that spurs your child's creativity. You can enroll your kids in a project like this, too, because we built pretty much everything in this room using simple MDF (Medium Density Fiberboard) and ordinary household objects. Oh, and imagination, of course.

The centerpiece of the room is a fabulous fantasy bed that I like to call the Christopher Lowell Cadillac Edition. The great thing about this bed is that you can customize it to your child's tastes. You can see how we put the bed together on page 166, but the design is very flexible. Because the rails of the bed are simple jigsaw cutouts, you can change the silhouette, then paint and accessorize to make anything from a pink Cadillac to a yellow racing car. In our case, we used tomato red for a real retro kick. This comes in handy when you're on Route 66.

What really adds authenticity to this car are the details. We found many of them by visiting auto supply stores and junkyards—another great expedition for kids. Take kids shopping for really cool and unusual objects they can choose themselves, then transform the purchases into part of their room décor.

Kids need a lot of shelf space to put all their toys, books, science projects, and miscellaneous treasures. That's why we created not only a great desk that has a ton of storage, but a full wall-length shelving unit. The modular construction of both pieces is similar. We designed the vertical rails in a flared tailfin shape that echoes the shape of the bed rails. Into the back of these upright pieces we cut channels into which the horizontal shelves can be fitted. So the shelves themselves are all one piece. This eliminates a lot of extra cutting and fitting. The desk has towers on either side extending both on top of and underneath the work surface. Sitting at this desk is like strapping yourself into the cockpit of your own private jet. I think I could do my homework here! Again, we used the red for these units, and accented the shelves in a nifty green.

We created wainscoting from a roll of speckled vinyl flooring, capping off with fiber optic rope lights. It's a sort of 1950s diner-inspired neon effect. Staying with this diner feeling, we laid an inexpensive black and white tile on the floor. It's durable and easy to clean, plus it's got that finish-line-flag look. With the theme now well established, we really went over the top. Take the lighted side table: How's that for a whimsical alien touch? We also strung up some great teardrop lights from Ikea, then took some plain old shades and turned them into flying saucers. This room is ready for takeoff! Your child will enjoy it every day, at least until it's time to get a *real* driver's license.

OPPOSITE Can't you imagine yourself doing homework at this desk? The design could also be used in a kitchen or even an office.

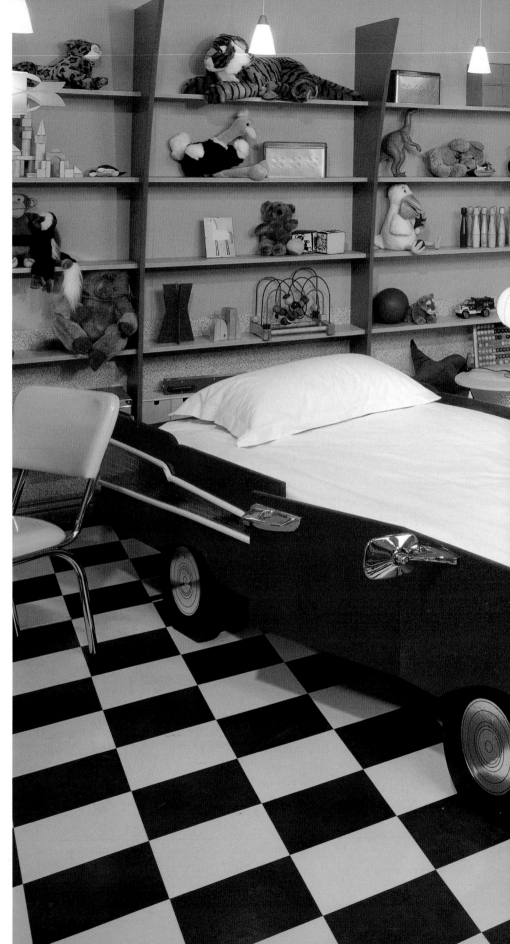

During

ABOVE Is it furniture or a UFO? The components of this side table are pretty straightforward: three plastic salad bowls, three soup ladles, and a piece of plywood. We reverse-stacked the salad bowls and covered the top with a plywood disk fitted with a flashing light. The soup ladles have been bolted to the bowls to serve as legs.

RIGHT Check out this room. Not only is it a place where kids will want to spend time, but it is also a practical living space, too, with plenty of shelves. It's always good design when you attend to function and storage.

"cadillac" bed

THE CHRISTOPHER LOWELL EDITION

Even though this bed looks complicated, most of the components are simple wood boxes held together with wood glue and screws. If you decide to stain the bed, you should build it with plywood. But as we really wanted to play up the bright, glossy paint job on the car, we used MDF (Medium Density Fiberboard) for easy sanding and painting. Add to the authenticity of the look by installing real car door handles and chrome side mirrors purchased from an auto junkyard.

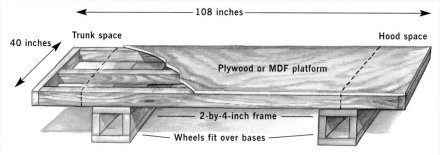

Four 4-by-8-foot sheets ¾-inch MDF
   (Medium Density Fiberboard) or
   plywood

2-by-4s

8 chrome piano hinges

Adhesive-backed silver foil paper

Plastic light fixture grid

2 headlights

2 car door handles

2 chrome auto side mirrors

Wood glue

Wood screws

Sandpaper

Paint: red high-gloss enamel, silver,
   white, and black

Paintbrushes

Power table saw and jigsaw

Power drill

Hammer

1. Make a frame for the bed platform consisting of 2-by-4s. Attach a platform of MDF or plywood to the top of the frame. To fit a twin-size mattress plus the hood and trunk of the car, the platform should measure 108 inches long by 40 inches wide. The frame should sit atop 2 rectangular plywood base boxes, located approximately where the front and back wheels of the car will be.

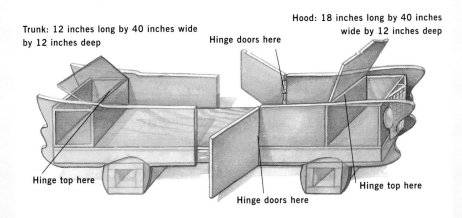

Trunk: 12 inches long by 40 inches wide by 12 inches deep

Hood: 18 inches long by 40 inches wide by 12 inches deep

Hinge doors here

Hinge top here

Hinge top here

Hinge doors here

2. Draw an outline of the sides onto MDF or plywood, making the top edge of the sides slightly higher than the top of the mattress. Cut out the sides with a jigsaw, or have them cut to your template by your lumber store. Cut the doors, separating each side into a front, a door, and a back section. Attach the front and back sides to the bed frame with wood glue and screws. Hang the doors from piano hinges on the side edge toward the front of the car. Construct 2 four-sided wood boxes for hood and trunk storage. Hinge the tops of the boxes with piano hinges. Secure the boxes to the car platform and sides.

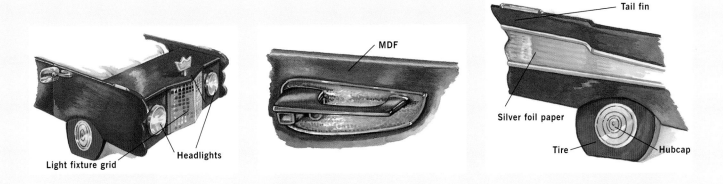

Light fixture grid

Headlights

MDF

Tail fin

Silver foil paper

Tire

Hubcap

3. Sand and paint the car. Attach a plastic grid to the front in a V shape and glue headlights on either side.

4. Glue or screw Glue or screw chrome door handles onto each door. We put a mounting plate of painted MDF underneath our handles.

5. For the tail fins, apply silver foil paper and paint. Paint the hubcaps silver, then draw on the tires with permanent marker.

the seven layers of design

PAINT AND ARCHITECTURE

Paint is one of the most effective and inexpensive ways to add substance, warmth, and "theme" to any room. But remember this golden rule: Paint the ceiling too. A touch of molding adds architecture to a room and value to your property.

INSTALLED FLOORING

Anything that runs from wall to wall, such as wood, tile, or carpet, completes the shell of the room. Choose something neutral in color. Furniture will interrupt these expanses, so be sure to consider how much of the floor you are going to see.

HIGH-TICKET UPHOLSTERY

The fabric on sofas, club chairs, and settees should be textural and solid rather than busy motifs that might be costly to change later when you tire of them. To avoid this pattern trap, reserve accent fabric for the next layer.

ACCENT FABRICS

Accent fabrics are those drapes, pillows, runners, and table toppers that help bring a room alive. Because they are more affordable to replace, they can be changed seasonally or when the pattern becomes dated. Area rugs are also part of this layer and are ideal centerpieces for conversation groupings.

THE NONUPHOLSTERED SURFACES

We call these the workhorses of the room. Tables, desks, bookcases, and armoires all help make a room functional, as well as provide storage. If your seating is clustered in a conversation grouping in the center of your room, the wall can then be left free for these necessary pieces. Remember: The human form needs only 18 to 20 inches between items to comfortably navigate a room, so when choosing a coffee table, go as big as you can.

Layer 5

ACCESSORIES

This layer includes wall art, vases, artwork, mirrors, and just about any decorative tabletop piece. Think in terms of fewer large-scale items rather than an abundance of small ones, which can easily get absorbed into the room and create "room dandruff."

Layer 6

PLANTS AND LIGHTING

These two elements are combined to create shadows, lending an air of intimacy to a room. As much light should be coming from the floor as from the ceiling; an uplight under a large-scale tree casts dramatic ceiling shadows, while task lamps add function and decoration to a space. The flicker of candlelight adds a warmly romantic and cozy feeling. Recess, spot, or track lighting helps draw the eye to specific objects of interest. Washed light on richly colored walls accentuates surface texture and artwork.

Layer 7

For a more detailed explanation of these layers and how to use them, please refer to *Christopher Lowell's 7 Layers of Design: Fearless, Fabulous Decorating,* available in bookstores or online at www.christopherlowell.com.

resources

ALTHOUGH we built a lot of the furniture and accessories you see in these room makeovers, sometimes we like to go shopping, too. I thought you'd like to know where we find all the other great stuff you see in these pages. A listing of phone numbers and websites follows this list. You can find even more information on my website, www.christopherlowell.com.

ONE ROOM IN FOUR

Paint: Christopher Lowell Designer Paint (walls and ceiling: Drizzled Syrup; trim: Navy Bean)

Furniture & Lighting: Expressions Custom Furniture

Accessories: Burlington Coat Factory; IKEA; Tesserae Designs

FOUR ROOMS IN ONE

Paint: Circle Wall/Joe Fenzel, D.A.L.A.

Furniture: IKEA

Fabric: Calico Corners

Accessories: Blagg's; Linens 'n Things

Lighting: Charles Swanson; Lamps Plus

THEATER LIVING

Furniture: City Designs

Fabric: Waverly

Murals: Jeff Raum

MOROCCAN MYSTIQUE

Paint: Christopher Lowell Designer Paint (walls and ceiling: Clay Cotta; trim: Navy Bean)

Accessories: Cost Plus World Market

Fabric: Waverly

MARTINI LOUNGE

Furniture: City Designs; IKEA

Fabric: Calico Corners

Accessories: Cost Plus World Market; IKEA

Lighting: Lamps Plus

DECO LIVING

Paint: Christopher Lowell Designer Paint (walls: Peppercorn; ceiling: Misted Thyme; trim: Iced Pear)

Flooring: Alloc

Accessories: Van Dyke's Restorers

Wood: Wood Promotion Network

Plants: Maui Blooms; Trees International

Lighting: Scott Jilson/Haute Couture Lamps

BATHROOM:

Paint: Christopher Lowell Designer Paint (walls and ceiling: Claret & Cream: trim: Black)

Accessories: Burlington Coat Factory; IKEA

DOWN-BY-SEA

Paint: Christopher Lowell Designer Paint (walls: Walnut Shell; ceiling: Smoked Trout; trim: Navy Bean)

Fabric: Calico Corners

Bedding: Linens 'n Things

Bed Canopy: Mombassa Bed Canopies

Accessories: Cost Plus World Market; IKEA; Pier One Imports

Lighting: Lamps Plus

ALL ABOARD

Paint: Christopher Lowell Designer Paint (walls: Creamed Cabbage; trim: Navy Bean)

Blinds: 3 Day Blinds

Fabric: Calico Corners

Accessories: Cost Plus World Market; Expressions Custom Furniture; IKEA

SANCTUARY BY THE SHORE

Paint: Christopher Lowell Designer Paint (walls: Steamed Oatmeal; trim: Navy Bean)

Furniture: Expressions Custom Furniture

Bedding: Christopher Lowell Collection, Burlington Coat Factory

Accessories: Cost Plus World Market; IKEA; Stanley Mirrors

SOUTH SEA HAVEN

Paint: Christopher Lowell Designer Paint (walls: Dried Marjoram; ceiling: Cream of Mushroom; trim: Arrow Root)

Blinds: 3 Day Blinds

Fabric: Calico Corners

Accessories: Van Dyke's Restorers

Lighting: Tom Andres/Shell Lamps

FOYER EYES ONLY AND WIDE-OPEN SPACES

Paint: Christopher Lowell Designer Paint (walls: Pumpkin Pie; ceiling: Cream of Mushroom; trim: Arrow Root)

Fabric: Calico Corners

Accessories: The Bombay Company

POP TARTZ

Furniture: Harry's Furniture

Accessories: Cost Plus World Market; IKEA

RETRO CHIC

Flooring: Westling Design

Furniture: American Leather

Accessories: Cost Plus World Market; IKEA

Lighting: Lamps Plus

BELLY UP TO THE BAR

Paint: Christopher Lowell Designer Paint (walls: Pumpkin Pie, Deep Lowell Lavender & Baked Artichoke; ceiling: Smoked Trout; trim: Gold)

Upholstered Walls: Thomas Gil

Furniture & Fabrics: Flexsteel

Accessories: Burlington Coat Factory; Conso Tassels; Cost Plus World Market; Loose Ends; Stanley Mirrors; Van Dyke's Restorers

Lighting: Robert Abbey Lamps

FAMILY ONLINE

Paint: Christopher Lowell Designer Paint (walls: Baked Artichoke, Pumpkin Pie, Clay Cotta, & Deep Lowell Lavender; ceiling: Smoked Trout)

Furniture & Fabrics: Flexsteel; Kathy Ireland Home Collection

Work Centers: Sauder

Accessories: Burlington Coat Factory; Cost Plus World Market; Stanley Mirrors

Lighting: Robert Abbey Lamps

TEAHOUSE TERRIFIC

Paint: Christopher Lowell's Designer Paint (walls: Baked Artichoke, Pumpkin Pie, Smoked Trout & Clay Cotta; ceiling: Smoked Trout)

Desktop: Formica Corporation

Furniture: Herman Miller

Accessories: Loose Ends; Burlington Coat Factory

Lighting: Progress Lighting

ZEN-SATIONAL OFFICE

Paint: Christopher Lowell Designer Paint (Office #1 walls: Baked Artichoke & Deep Lowell Lavender; office #2 walls: Pumpkin Pie, Baked Artichoke & Clay Cotta; ceilings: Smoked Trout)

Furniture: Herman Miller; McDowell Craig Office Furniture

Desk Top: Formica Corporation

Fabric: Flexsteel

Accessories: Burlington Coat Factory; Cost Plus World Market; IKEA

Lighting: Robert Abbey Lamps

PARTY ALFRESCO

Umbrella: Ken Parker Designs

Mosaics: Dan Collins Mosaics

Stencil: Jan Dressler Stencils

Accessories: Weber Grills and Accessories

Plants: Ecke

THE ART OF DISGUISE

Murals: Jeff Raum

Accessories: Illuminations; Weber Grills and Accessories

Plants: Ecke

IN TRANSIT AND SOLAR SANCTUARY

Conservatory: Four Seasons Sunrooms

Flooring: Alloc

Furniture/Iron Work: Emanuele's House of Iron; Kathy Ireland World Wide

Accessories: F. W. Ritter and Sons; Oriental Weavers of America; Penpoint Graphics

Plants: Trees International

GOURMET UPGRADE

Paint: Christopher Lowell Designer Paint (walls: Dusted Mint; ceiling: Navy Bean)

Flooring: Alloc

Appliances: Jenn-Air

Appliance Covers: Frigo Designs

Accessories: Cost Plus World Market; IKEA

KITCHEN À LA CARTE

Furniture: Expressions Custom Furniture

Accessories: Arte de Mexico; Calphalon; Cost Plus World Market; IKEA; Pier One Imports

Tile: Bolivar Tile

Appliance Coverings: Frigo Design

SWEET DREAMS

Paint: Christopher Lowell Designer Paint (walls: Dried Rosemary; ceiling: Cream of Mushroom; trim: Arrowroot)

Stencils: Susan Pierce

Fabric: Calico Corners

Accessories: IKEA

GO KID GO

Accessories: IKEA

Wood: Wood Promotion Network

contact information

Alloc Original: 877-DO-ALLOC: www.alloc.com

American Leather: 972-296-9599; www.americanleather.com

Tom Andrews: 323-913-3946

Arte de Mexico: 818-753-4559; www.artedemexico.com

Blagg's: 323-661-9011

Bolivar Tile: 626-449-8453

The Bombay Company: 800-829-7789; www.bombayco.com

Burlington Coat Factory: 609-387-7800; www.coat.com

Calico Corners: 800-213-6366; www.calicocorners.com

Calphalon: 800-809-PANS; www.calphalon.com

Christopher Lowell Collection, Burlington Coat Factory: 609-387-7800; www.coat.com

Christopher Lowell Designer Paint Collection: www.christopherlowellpaint.com

City Designs: 310-202-8211

Conso Products Company: 800-845-2341; www.conso.com

Cost Plus World Market: 510-893-7300; www.costplus.com

Dan Collins Mosaics: 310-390-4232

Don Delino/Painters Plus: 310-798-0450

Paul Ecke Ranch: 800-468-ECKE;
www.ecke.com

Emanuele's House of Iron:
818-753-5670

Expressions Custom Furniture:
800-544-4519;
www.expressionsfurniture.com

F. W. Ritter and Sons:
800-424-1949; www.claypots.com

Flexsteel: www.flexsteel.com

Formica Corporation:
800-FORMICA; www.formica.com

Four Seasons Sunrooms:
800-FOURSEASONS;
www.four-seasons-sunrooms.com

Joe Fenzel, D.A.L.A.:
818-997-0116

Frigo Design: 800-836-8746

Thomas Gil: 626-201-4904

Harry's Furniture: 310-559-7863

IKEA: 800-434-IKEA;
www.ikea.com

Illuminations: 800-621-2998;
www.illuminations.com

Jan Dressler Stencils:
888-656-4515;
www.dresslerstencils.com

Jenn-Air: 800-688-1100;
www.jennair.com

Kathy Ireland Home Collection,
Kathy Ireland World Wide:
310-557-2700;
www.kathyireland.com

Ken Parker Designs: 760-320-6222

Lamps Plus: 800-782-1967;
www.lampsplus.com

Linens 'n Things: 866-568-7378;
www.lnt.com

Loose Ends: 503-390-2348;
www.looseends.com

Maui Blooms: 800-451-0618;
www.mauiblooms.net

Mombassa Bed Canopies:
800-611-2345

McDowell Craig Office Furniture:
877-921-2100;
www.mcdowellcraig.com

Herman Miller: 888-443-4357;
www.hermanmiller.com

Oriental Weavers of America: 706-
277-9666; www.owarug.com

Penpoint Graphics: 877-736-0900;
www.penpoint.com

Pier One Imports: 800-245-4595;
www.pierone.com

Susan Pierce: 562-594-6214;
spierce@adelphia.net

Progress Lighting: 864-599-6000;
www.progresslighting.com

Robert Abbey Inc.: 828-322-3480;
www.robertabbey.com

Jeff Raum: 310-789-4449;
www.jeffraumstencils.com

Sauder Woodworking:
800-523-3987; www.sauder.com

Scott Jilson/Haute Couture Lamps:
603-431-9088;
www.scottjilson.com

Stanley Mirrors: 800-STANLEY;
www.stanleyworks.com

Stroheim & Romann: 718-706-7000;
www.stroheim.com

Charles Swanson: 310-394-4045

Tesserae Designs: 949-574-9259

3 Day Blinds: 800-800-3DAY;
www.3day.com

Trees International: 888-873-3799;
www.treesinternational.com

Van Dyke's Restorers:
800-558-1234; www.vandykes.com

Waverly: www.waverly.com

Weber Grills and Accessories:
800-446-1071; www.weber.com

Westling Design: 800-690-8007;
www.westlingdesign.com

Wood Promotion Network/
Be Constructive:
www.beconstructive.com

index

the wrap

MY FIRST BOOK, *Christopher Lowell's 7 Layers of Design,* provided a sequential road map to help you accomplish the physical process of decorating your home. It told you how to stay on budget and, more important, out of overwhelm. I know that it resonated with you, because it's now in its ninth printing. My hope is that as you've perused this new book, it has taken you even further into the spiritual process of looking at how you live and considering new creative possibilities.

Ironically, I began this book in response to the many readers and viewers who wrote to express their concerns after the horrific shootings in various schools in the country. What they expressed to me was a desire to find more protected neighborhoods that could assure their children's safety—from each other. It was then that I realized that both we and our children had lost something very important: our ability to dream. What's more, as a result of their own daily preoccupations, many parents either did not have the skills to nurture their children's dreams or even the ability to recognize them.

I felt the need to outline a new mission, one that integrated the aspects of my work that you told me were important to you. As a result, I literally locked myself in a hotel room for a full week, free from the distractions of my hectic schedule and even the comforts of my own home. There I outlined my new mission, The Dare to Dream Project, which has already gained tremendous support and will in fact result in a full-blown theatrical production to tour major theaters across America. Talk about my life coming full circle!

Little did I know then that the tragedy of September 11, 2001, was looming in the near future; the horrific events of that day may have irrevocably altered life in the United States. It seems a shame that it took a tragedy of that great magnitude to make us Americans wake up—to force us to set aside our differences and come together as a nation. Look around you now. As we begin to strengthen our sense of national pride and patriotism, rekindling the values and priorities that this country was founded on, perhaps you can see how important it is that this emerging new spirit begins at home.

After all, it is the nucleus of home that can nourish us, remind us of what we hold dear, and provide the daily arena in which to celebrate the very essence of what it is to be human. It's our private place away from the world's craziness, where we can explore who we are and who we want to be, challenge our sense of personal creativity, and simply dream. By surrounding ourselves with those whom we cherish and the things we love, our chances of having a satisfying life increases. By truly experiencing joy now and not postponing our happiness for a later date, we can make room for a life we never dreamed we'd have. So ask yourself, "Are dreams worth it?"

If you are feeling in need of support, I hope you'll be part of our incredible television audience every weekday. If you need to chat, find information, or simply bond with like-minded people, you should log on to our website, www.christopherlowell.com.

And remember, you're not alone—you can do it!